# My Samsung
# Galaxy™ Nexus™

Craig James Johnston

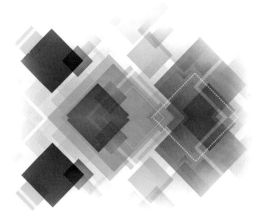

800 East 96th Street,
Indianapolis, Indiana 46240 USA

# My Samsung Galaxy™ Nexus™

## Copyright © 2013 by Pearson Education, Inc.

ISBN-13: 978-0-7897-4946-8

ISBN-10: 7-7897-4946-7

Library of Congress Cataloging-in-Publication Data is on file and available upon request.

Printed in the United States of America

First Printing: July 2012

## Trademarks

## Warning and Disclaimer

## Bulk Sales

Que Publishing offers excellent discounts on this book when ordered in quantity for bulk purchases or special sales. For more information, please contact

**U.S. Corporate and Government Sales**

**1-800-382-3419**

**corpsales@pearsontechgroup.com**

For sales outside of the U.S., please contact

**International Sales**

**international@pearsoned.com**

**Editor-in-Chief**
Greg Wiegand

**Acquisitions Editor**
Michelle Newcomb

**Development Editor**
Charlotte Kughen, The Wordsmithery LLC

**Managing Editor**
Kristy Hart

**Senior Project Editor**
Lori Lyons

**Indexer**
Erika Millen

**Proofreader**
Language Logistics, LLC

**Technical Editor**
Christian Kenyeres

**Editorial Assistant**
Cindy Teeters

**Book Designer**
Anne Jones

**Compositor**
Bronkella Publishing

# Contents at a Glance

# Table of Contents

## 2  Using the Phone and Google Voice    **65**

## 5  Emailing                           159

My Samsung Galaxy Nexus

# About the Author

**Craig James Johnston** has been involved with technology since his high school days at Glenwood High in Durban, South Africa, when his school was given some Apple ][ Europluses. From that moment technology captivated him, and he has owned, supported, evangelized, and written about it.

Craig has been involved in designing and supporting large-scale enterprise networks with integrated email and directory services since 1989. He has held many different IT-related positions in his career ranging from sales support engineer to mobile architect for a 40,000-smartphone infrastructure at a large bank.

In addition to designing and supporting mobile computing environments, Craig co-hosts the CrackBerry.com podcast, as well as guest hosting on other podcasts including iPhone and iPad Live podcasts. You can see Craig's previously published work in his books *Professional BlackBerry*, and many books in the *My* series, including *My BlackBerry Curve*, *My Palm Pre*, *My Nexus One*, *My DROID* (first and second editions), *My Motorola Atrix 4G*, *My BlackBerry PlayBook*, and *My HTC EVO 3D*.

Craig also enjoys high-horsepower, high-speed vehicles and tries very hard to keep to the speed limit while driving them.

Originally from Durban, South Africa, Craig has lived in the United Kingdom, the San Francisco Bay Area, and New Jersey, where he now lives with his wife, Karen, and a couple of cats.

Craig would love to hear from you. Feel free to contact Craig about your experiences with *My Samsung Galaxy Nexus* at http://www.CraigsBooks.info.

All comments, suggestions, and feedback are welcome, including positive and negative.

# Dedication

*"Any sufficiently advanced technology is indistinguishable from magic."*
—Arthur C. Clark

# Acknowledgments

I would like to express my deepest gratitude to the following people on the *My Samsung Galaxy Nexus* team, who all worked extremely hard on this book.

Michelle Newcomb, my acquisitions editor, who worked with me to give this project an edge, as well as technical editor Christian Keyneres, development editor Charlotte Kughen, project editor Lori Lyons, indexer Cheryl Lenser, compositor Tricia Bronkella, and proofreader Chrissy White.

I would also like to thank Chantal de Maudave for allowing me to use her face for the special effects part of the video chapter.

Finally, I'd like to thank Kerry Harrington from Weber Shandwick for helping with the Verizon version of the Galaxy Nexus, and Negri Electronics for providing early purchase access to the GSM version.

# We Want to Hear from You!

As the reader of this book, *you* are our most important critic and commentator. We value your opinion and want to know what we're doing right, what we could do better, what areas you'd like to see us publish in, and any other words of wisdom you're willing to pass our way.

We welcome your comments. You can email or write to let us know what you did or didn't like about this book—as well as what we can do to make our books better.

*Please note that we cannot help you with technical problems related to the topic of this book.*

When you write, please be sure to include this book's title and author as well as your name and email address. We will carefully review your comments and share them with the author and editors who worked on the book.

Email:   feedback@quepublishing.com

Mail:    Que Publishing
         ATTN: Reader Feedback
         800 East 96th Street
         Indianapolis, IN 46240 USA

# Reader Services

Visit our website and register this book at quepublishing.com/register for convenient access to any updates, downloads, or errata that might be available for this book.

Drag to launch the camera

Drag to unlock

# Prologue

In this chapter, you learn about the external features of the Galaxy Nexus and the basics of getting started with the Android operating system. Topics include the following:

- → The Galaxy Nexus external features
- → Fundamentals of Android 4 (Ice Cream Sandwich)
- → First time setup
- → Installing synchronization software

# Getting to Know Your Galaxy Nexus

Let's start by getting to know more about your Galaxy Nexus by examining the external features, device features, and how Google's latest operating system, Android 4.0 (or Ice Cream Sandwich), works.

One important thing to remember about any Android smartphone bearing the Nexus name is that it is a pure Android phone with no wireless carrier or vendor modifications. Google, the company that makes Android, commissions Nexus phones to have the latest features and run the latest version of Google's Android operating system, in this case Android 4, but Google insists that it is the pure, unchanged version of Android.

## The Galaxy Nexus External Features

Becoming familiar with the external features of your Galaxy Nexus is a good place to start because you will be using them often. This chapter also covers some of the technical specifications of your

Galaxy Nexus, including the touch screen and camera. There are four versions of the Galaxy Nexus: Two that work on the global GSM networks (one of them with a logo on the back for NTT Docomo), and two that run on CDMA networks operated by U.S. carriers Verizon and Sprint.

The Global GSM version of the Galaxy Nexus is also known by its official model name of Samsung GT-i9250, the NTT Docomo GSM version is called the Samsung SC-04D, the Verizon CDMA version is known as the Samsung SCH-i515, and the Sprint CDMA version is the Samsung SPHL-700.

# Front

**Proximity sensor**    Detects when you place your Galaxy Nexus against your ear to talk, which causes it to turn off the screen to prevent any buttons from being pushed inadvertently.

**Light sensor**    Adjusts the brightness of the screen based on the brightness of the ambient light.

**Earpiece**    Hold against your ear while on a call.

**Indicator light**    Indicates new events (such as missed calls or new email). The light can be any color combination of red, green, or blue (RGB) so different apps can use different colors of alerts.

**Front camera**    5.0 Megapixel front-facing camera that you can use for video chat, taking self-portraits, and even unlocking your Galaxy Nexus using your face.

**Touchscreen**    The Galaxy Nexus has a 4.65" 720X1280 pixel Super AMOLED HD (Super Active-Matrix Organic Light-Emitting Diode) screen that incorporates capacitive touch.

**Back button**    Touch to go back one screen when using an application or menu. This virtual button is actually on the screen.

**Recent Apps button**    Touch to see a list of recently used apps and switch between them. This virtual button is actually on the screen.

**Home button**    Touch to go to the Home screen. The application that you are using continues to run in the background. This virtual button is actually on the screen.

# Back

**Back cover removal point**

**Noise-cancelling microphone**

**5 Megapixel camera with autofocus**

**LED camera flash**

**Speaker**

**3.5mm Headphone jack**

**MHL-compliant Micro-USB port**

**5 Megapixel camera with autofocus**   Takes clear pictures close-up or far away.

**LED (Light Emitting Diode) camera flash**   Helps to illuminate the surroundings when taking pictures in low light.

**Speaker**   Produces audio when speakerphone is in use. Place your Galaxy Nexus on a hard surface for the best audio reflection.

**Noise-cancelling microphone**    Used in conjunction with the regular micro-phone on phone calls to reduce background noise. This microphone is also used when you record videos.

**3.5mm headphone jack**    Used with third-party headsets so you can enjoy music and talk on the phone.

**MHL-compliant Micro-USB port**    Used to synchronize your Galaxy Nexus to your desktop computer and charge it, but because it is Mobile High-definition Link (MHL) compliant, you can use it to play movies on your TV via HDMI using a special cable or dock.

**Back cover removal point**    Insert your fingernail and pull to remove the back cover.

## Left Side

Volume up/down buttons

**Volume up/down buttons**    Control the audio volume on calls and while playing audio and video.

# Right Side

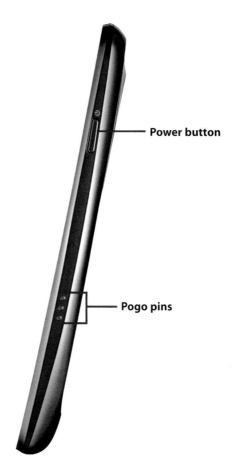

Power button

Pogo pins

**Power button**  Press once to wake your Galaxy Nexus. Press and hold for one second to reveal a menu of choices. The choices enable you to put your Galaxy Nexus into silent mode, airplane mode, or power it off completely.

**Pogo pins**  Use with accessories and docks to automatically start certain applications and charge your Galaxy Nexus. For example, a vehicle dock could automatically launch the Navigation app.

## Main Differences Between the Four Galaxy Nexus Versions

Every aspect of the four versions of the Galaxy Nexus is the same with the exception of the size and mobile technologies supported.

The Global GSM version of the Galaxy Nexus (the GT-i9250) and the NTT Docomo GSM version (SC-04D) is 135.5mm × 67.9mm × 8.9mm and weighs 135g, whereas the Verizon CDMA version (SCH-i515) and the Sprint CDMA version (SPHL-700) is 135.5mm × 67.9mm × 9.5mm and weighs 150g.

The Global GSM and GSM NTT Docomo versions support the GSM 850/900/1800/1900 2G networks and the HSDPA 850/900/1700/1900/2100 3G networks, whereas the CDMA versions supports the CDMA 800/1900 2G networks, the CDMA2000 1xEV-DO 3G network. The Verizon version supports the LTE 700 4G network; the Sprint version supports the LTE 1900 4G network.

# First-Time Setup

Before setting up your new Samsung Galaxy Nexus it is advisable you have a Google account. This is because your Galaxy Nexus running Android is tightly integrated into Google and enables you to store your content in the Google cloud, including any books and music you buy or movies you rent. If you do not already have a Google account, head to https://accounts.google.com on your desktop computer and sign up for one.

1. Touch and hold the Power button until you see the animation start playing after you have inserted the SIM card (non-Verizon only) and battery.

2. Touch to change your location if needed.

3. Touch Start.

**Touch to make an emergency call**

4.  Touch Sign in.

5.  Enter your Google account user-name (which is your Gmail email address).

6.  Enter your Google account pass-word.

7.  Touch Sign In.

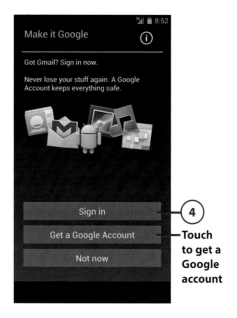

**Touch to get a Google account**

8. Check this box if you are switching from a previous Android phone and want to move all of your apps and settings to your new Galaxy Nexus.

9. Check this box if you want your apps and settings to be backed up to the Google cloud.

10. Touch Next.

11. Check this box if you are okay with Google collecting information about your geographic location at any time. Although Google keeps this information safe, if you are concerned about privacy rights you should uncheck this box.

12. Check this box if you are okay with Google using your geographic location for Google searches and other Google services.

13. Touch Next.

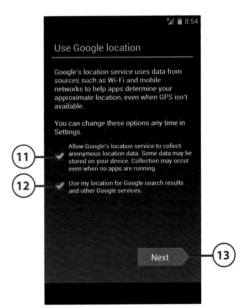

**14.** Enter your first name (given name) and last name (surname).

**15.** Touch Next.

**16.** Touch Finish.

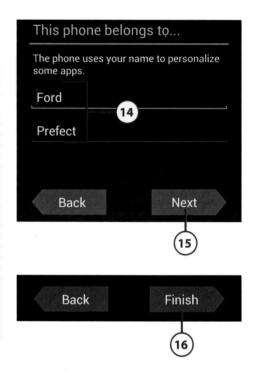

# Fundamentals of Android 4

Your Galaxy Nexus is run by an operating system called Android. Android was created by Google to run on any smartphone, and there are quite a few phones that run on Android today. Your Galaxy Nexus uses the latest version of Android, called Android 4 (or Ice Cream Sandwich). Let's go over how to use Android 4.

# The Unlock Screen

If you haven't used your Galaxy
Nexus for a while, the screen goes
blank to conserve battery power.
Here is how to interact with the Lock
screen.

1. Press the Power button to wake
   up your Galaxy Nexus.

2. Slide the padlock icon to the right
   to unlock Galaxy Nexus.

3. Slide the padlock icon to the left
   to launch the camera app.

## Work with Notifications on the Lock Screen

With Android 4 you can work with
notifications right on the Lock
screen. If you see notifications in
the Notification bar, pull down
the Notification bar to view and
clear them. Touching a notification takes you straight to the app
that created them. Read more
about the Notification bar later in
this section.

## Answer a Call from the Lock Screen

If your Galaxy Nexus is locked
when a call comes in, the padlock icon becomes a phone icon.
Drag it to the right to answer the
incoming call. Drag it to the left to
ignore the incoming call and send
it straight to Voice Mail. Drag it up
to send a text message (SMS) to
the caller.

**Notifications**

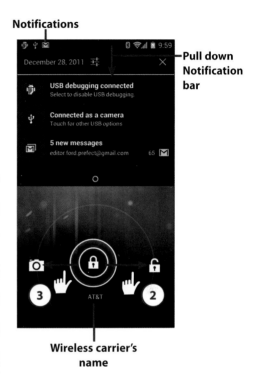

Pull down Notification bar

Wireless carrier's name

Slide up to send a text message

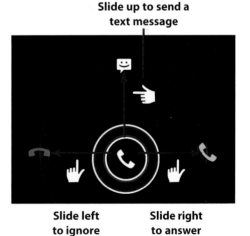

Slide left to ignore    Slide right to answer

# The Home Screen(s)

After you unlock your Galaxy Nexus, you are presented with the middle Home screen. Your Galaxy Nexus has five Home screens. The Home screens contain application shortcuts, a Launcher icon, Notification Bar, Shortcuts, Favorites Tray, and widgets.

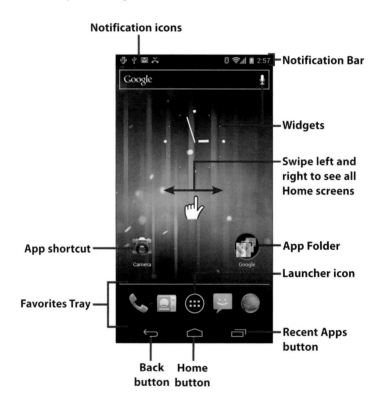

**Notification Bar**    The Notification Bar shows information about Bluetooth, Wi-Fi, and cellular coverage, as well as the battery level and time. The Notification Bar also serves as a place where apps can alert or notify you using notification icons.

**Notification icons**    Notification icons appear in the Notification Bar when an app needs to alert or notify you of something. For example, the Phone app can show the missed call icon indicating that you missed a call.

## Working with Notifications

To interact with notifications that appear in the Notification Bar, place your finger above the top of the screen and drag it down to reveal the notifications. Touch the blue X to clear all notifications or swipe each individual notification off the screen to the left or right to clear them one by one.

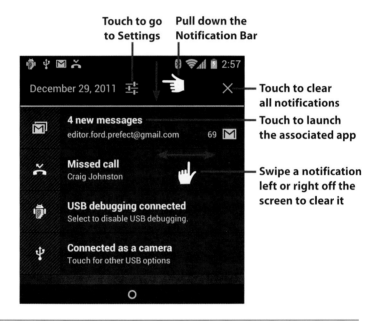

**Widgets**  Widgets are applications that run right on the Home screens. They are specially designed to provide functionality and real-time information. An example of a widget is one that shows the current weather or provides search capability. You can move and resize widgets.

**App shortcut**  Touching an app shortcut launches the associated app.

## Creating App Shortcuts

Touch the Launcher icon to see all of your apps. Touch and hold on the app you want to make a shortcut for. After the Home screens appear, drag the app shortcut to where you want it on the Home screen, drag it to an App Folder to add it to the folder, or drag it left or right off the screen to move it between Home screens. Release the icon to place it.

**Touch and hold the app icon** ———

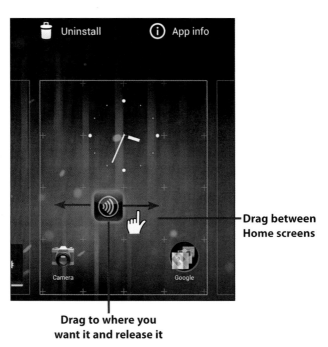

**Drag between Home screens**

**Drag to where you want it and release it**

**App Folders** App Folders are groups of apps that you can use to organize apps and declutter your screen.

# Creating App Folders

To create a new App Folder, simply drag one app shortcut onto another one. An App Folder is created automatically. To name your new App Folder, touch the folder to open it and touch Unnamed Folder to enter your own name.

**Drag icons onto each other to make folders**

**Touch to name your App Folder**
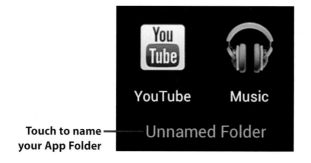

**Favorites Tray**    The Favorites Tray is visible on all five Home screens. You can drag apps to the Favorites Tray so that they are available no matter which Home screen you are looking at. Apps in the Favorites Tray can be rearranged and removed.

**Launcher icon**    Touch to show application icons for all applications that you have installed on your Galaxy Nexus.

# The System Bar

Your Galaxy Nexus running Android 4 has no physical buttons. Instead it has an area of the screen set aside for virtual buttons. This new area is called the System Bar. The System Bar includes the Back, Home, and Recent Apps virtual buttons. When apps run, the Menu button virtual button is also visible.

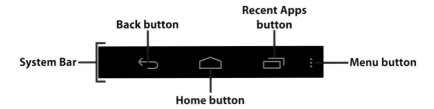

**System Bar**   Reserved area of the screen where virtual buttons are displayed.

**Back button**   Touch to go back one screen in an app or back one step while navigating Android.

**Home button**   Touch to exit what you are doing and return to the Home screen.

**Recent Apps button**   Touch to see your recently used apps, switch between them, and close them.

**Menu button**   Replaces the physical Menu button that was used with previous versions of Android and provides contextual actions. While apps are running, the Menu button normally appears in the System Bar but can sometimes appear in the top right of the screen.

## Vanishing System Bar

Some apps can dim or hide the System Bar to provide that little extra screen real estate. When this happens, the virtual buttons are still there, however, they are reduced to very dim dots.

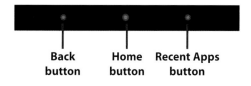

**Back**   **Home**   **Recent Apps**
**button**   **button**   **button**

# Using Your Touchscreen

Interacting with your Galaxy Nexus is done mostly by touching the screen—what's known as making gestures on the screen. You can touch, swipe, pinch, double-tap, and type.

**Touch**   To start an application, touch its icon. Touch a menu item to select it. Touch the letters of the onscreen keyboard to type.

**Touch and hold**   Touch and hold to interact with an object. For example, if you touch and hold a blank area of the Home screen, a menu pops up. If you touch and hold an icon, you can reposition it with your finger.

**Drag**   Dragging always starts with a touch and hold. For example, if you touch the Notification Bar, you can drag it down to read all of the notification messages.

**Swipe or slide**   Swipe or slide the screen to scroll quickly. To swipe or slide, move your finger across the screen quickly. Be careful not to touch and hold before you swipe or you will reposition something. You can also swipe to clear notifications or close apps when viewing the recent apps.

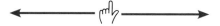

**Double-tap**   Double-tapping is like double-clicking a mouse on a desktop computer. Tap the screen twice in quick succession. For example, you can double-tap a web page to zoom in to part of that page.

**Pinch**   To zoom in and out of images and pages, place your thumb and forefinger on the screen. Pinch them together to zoom out or spread them apart to zoom in (unpinching). Applications such as Browser, Gallery, and Maps support pinching.

**Rotate the screen**   If you rotate your Galaxy Nexus from an upright position to being on its left or right side, the screen switches from portrait view to landscape view. Most applications honor the screen orientation. The Home screens and Launcher do not.

# Using Your Keyboard

Your Galaxy Nexus has a virtual (onscreen) keyboard for those times when you need to enter text. You may be a little wary of a keyboard that has no physical keys, but you will be pleasantly surprised at how well it works.

Some applications automatically show the keyboard when you need to enter text. If the keyboard does not appear, touch the area where you want to type and the keyboard slides up ready for use.

Double-tap to engage CAPS lock

Touch to capitalize the next character

Touch for numbers and symbols

Touch to speak the text

Touch to hide the keyboard

Using the virtual keyboard as you type, your Galaxy Nexus makes word suggestions. Think of this as similar to the spell checker you would see in a word processor. Your Galaxy Nexus uses a dictionary of words to guess what you are typing. If the word you were going to type is highlighted, touch space or period to select it. If you can see the word in the list but it is not highlighted, touch the word to select it.

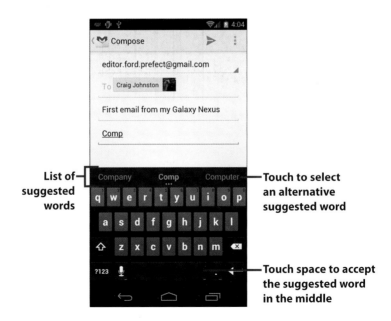

List of suggested words

Touch to select an alternative suggested word

Touch space to accept the suggested word in the middle

## Add Your Word

If you type a word that you know is correct, you can add it to your personal dictionary so that next time you type it, your Galaxy Nexus won't try to correct it. To do this, after you have typed the word, you see it as the middle suggested word. Touch the word once. Your word is underlined in red and listed in the suggested words area. Touch it one more time to add it to your personal dictionary.

**Touch to add your
word to the dictionary**

**Touch your word again
to complete the save**

To make the next letter you type a capital letter, touch the Shift key. To make all letters capitals (or CAPS), double-tap the Shift key to engage CAPS Lock. Touch Shift again to disengage CAPS Lock.

To type numbers or symbols, touch the Symbols key.

When on the Numbers and Symbols screen, touch the Symbols key to see extra symbols. Touch the ABC key to return to the regular keyboard.

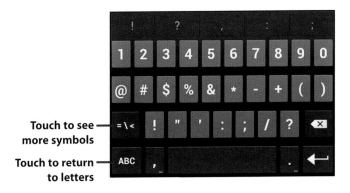

Touch to see more symbols

Touch to return to letters

## Quick Access to Symbols

If you want to type commonly used symbols, touch and hold the period key. A small window opens with those common symbols. Slide your finger over the symbol you want to type and lift it to type that symbol.

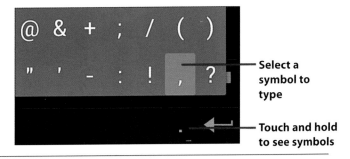

Select a symbol to type

Touch and hold to see symbols

To enter an accented character, touch and hold any vowel or the C, N, or S keys. A small window opens enabling you to select an accented or alternative character. Slide your finger over the accented character and lift your finger to type it.

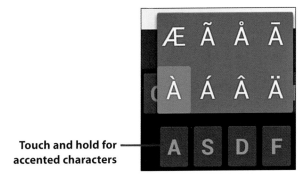

Touch and hold for accented characters

To reveal other alternative characters, touch and hold any other letter, number, or symbol.

## Want a Larger Keyboard?

Turn your Galaxy Nexus sideways to switch to a landscape keyboard. The landscape keyboard has larger keys and is easier to type on.

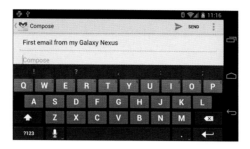

## Dictation: Speak Instead of Typing

Your Galaxy Nexus can turn your voice into text. It uses Google's speech recognition service, which means that you must have a connection to the cellular network or a Wi-Fi network in order to use it.

1. Touch the microphone key.

2. Wait until you see Listening and start speaking what you want to be typed. You can speak the punctuation by saying "comma," "question mark," "exclamation mark," or "exclamation point."

3. Touch Done to exit dictation mode.

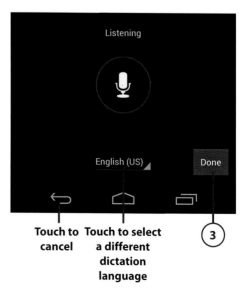

Touch to cancel    Touch to select a different dictation language

# Editing Text

After you enter text, you can edit it by cutting, copying, or pasting the text. Here is how to select and copy text and then paste over a word with the copied text.

1. While you are typing, touch and hold a word you want to copy.

2. Slide the blue end markers until you have selected all of the text you want to copy.

3. Touch to copy the text.

4. Touch and hold the word you want to paste over.

5. Touch Paste.

## Simpler Copy/Paste

You might want to just copy some text and paste it somewhere else instead of pasting it over a word. To do this, after you have copied the text, touch once in the text area, move the single blue marker to where you want to paste the text. Touch the blue marker again and touch Paste.

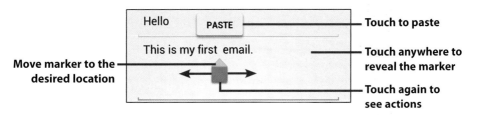

# Menus

Your Galaxy Nexus has two types of menus: Regular menus and Context menus. Let's go over what each one does.

Most applications have a Menu button. These enable you to make changes or take actions within that application. The Menu button can appear in the System Bar next to the Recent Apps button, on the top-right on the screen, or elsewhere in the app.

Touch the Menu button to reveal the App menu

A Context menu applies to an item on the screen. If you touch and hold something on the screen (in this example, a link on a web page), a Context menu appears. The items on the Context menu differ based on the type of object you touched.

Touch and hold a link to reveal the link Context menu

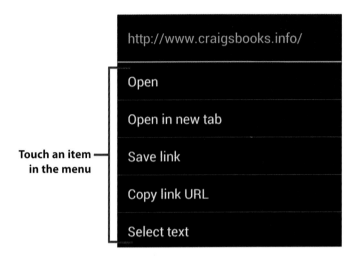

Touch an item
in the menu

# Switching Between Apps

As discussed earlier in this chapter, your Galaxy Nexus has a new button called the Recent Apps button. This button is always in the System Bar at the bottom of your screen. You can use this button to switch between apps, close apps, and force them to quit if they have stopped responding. Here is how.

1. Touch the Recent Apps button.

2. Scroll up and down the list of recent apps.

3. Swipe an app left or right off the screen to close it.

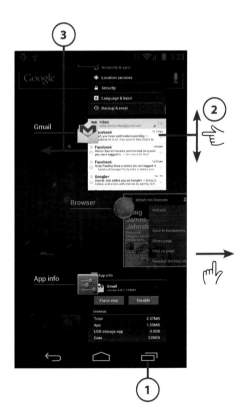

4. Touch and hold an app to reveal the menu.

5. Touch to force an app to close and see more information about the app.

# Installing Synchronization Software

Because your Galaxy Nexus is tightly integrated with Google and its services, all media that you purchase on your phone is stored in the Google cloud and accessible anywhere and anytime. However, you might have a lot of music on your computer already that you need to copy to your Google cloud and so you need to install the Google Music Manager software or the Android File Transfer app for your Mac to copy any file back and forth.

## Installing Android File Transfer (Apple Mac OSX)

You only need the Android File Transfer app when using a Samsung Android phone (such as your Galaxy Nexus) on an Apple Mac running OSX.

1. From your Mac, browse to http://www.android.com/filetransfer/ and download the Android File Transfer app.

**2.** Double-click the app in your Safari Downloads.

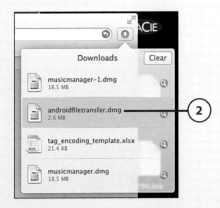

**3.** Drag the green Android to the Applications shortcut to install the app.

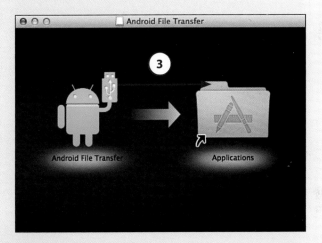

# Installing Google Music Manager (Apple Mac)

Don't install Google Music Manager unless you plan to upload files from your computer to the Google Music cloud.

**1.** Visit https://music.google.com/music/listen#manager_pl from your desktop web browser and log in to your Google account if prompted.

**2.** Click to download Music Manager.

3. Double-click the app in your Safari Downloads.

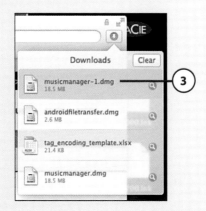

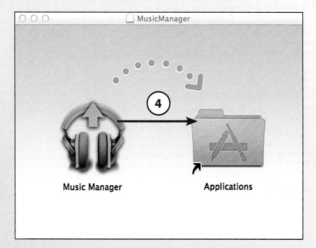

4. Drag the Music Manager icon to the Applications shortcut to install the app.

5. Double-click the Music Manager icon in the Applications folder.

6. Skip to the "Configuring Music Manager" section later in the chapter to complete the installation.

# Installing Google Music Manager (Windows)

Don't install Google Music Manager unless you plan to upload files from your computer to the Google Music cloud.

**1.** Visit https://music.google.com/music/listen#manager_pl from your desktop web browser and log in to your Google account if prompted.

**2.** Click to download Music Manager.

**3.** Double-click the app in your Downloads folder.

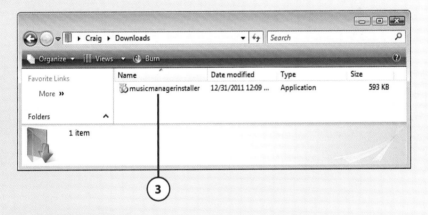

**4.** Skip to the "Configuring Music Manager" section later in the chapter to complete the installation.

# Configuring Music Manager (Windows and Apple Mac)

**1.** Click Continue.

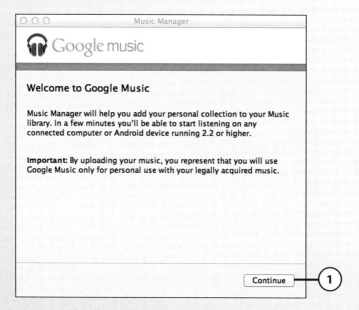

**2.** Enter your Google (Gmail) email address.

**3.** Enter your Google (Gmail) password.

**4.** Click Continue.

**5.** Choose where you keep your music.

**6.** Click Continue.

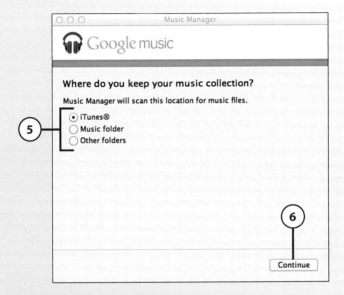

**7.** Choose whether to upload all of your music or just some of your playlists. Remember that you can only upload 20,000 songs for free. Skip to step 12 if you choose to upload all music.

**8.** Check if you want to also upload podcasts.

**9.** Click Continue.

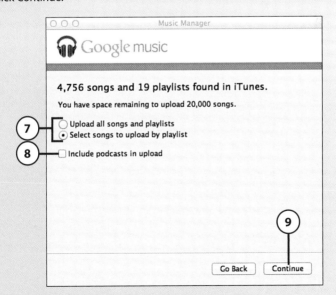

**10.** Select one or more playlists of music.

**11.** Click Continue.

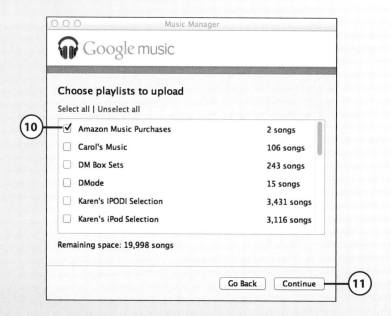

**12.** Choose whether you want to automatically upload any new music that is added to your computer.

**13.** Click Continue.

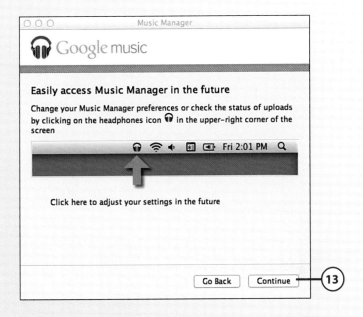

**14.** Click Close.

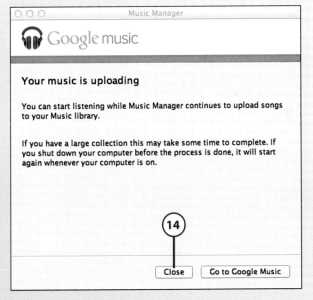

Add, search, and manage
your contacts

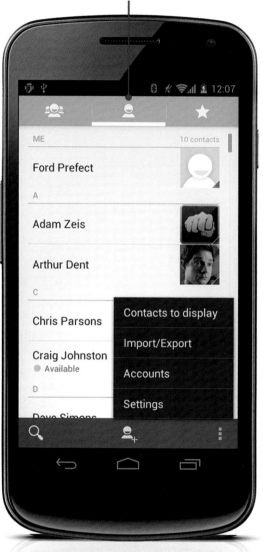

In this chapter, you learn about your Galaxy Nexus' most important application, People. You learn how to add contacts, synchronize contacts, join duplicate contacts together, and even how to add a contact to your Home screen. Topics include the following:

→ Importing contacts

→ Adding contacts

→ Synchronizing contacts

→ Creating favorite contacts

# People (Contacts)

On any smartphone the application for managing contacts is the most important because it is where you keep all of your contacts' information. On the Galaxy Nexus, this application is called People. It is the central hub for many activities such as calling and sending texts (SMS), multimedia files (MMS), or email. You can also synchronize your contacts from many online sites such as Facebook and Gmail, so as your friends change their Facebook profile pictures, their pictures on your Galaxy Nexus change, too. It's time to open People and look around.

# Adding Accounts

Before you look around the People application, try adding some accounts to synchronize contacts from. You already added your Google account when you set up your Galaxy Nexus in the Prologue chapter.

## Adding Facebook, Twitter, LinkedIn, and Other Accounts

To add accounts for your online services such as Facebook, Twitter, LinkedIn, and so on, install the apps for those services from Google Play. Please see how to install apps in Chapter 10, "Working with Android Applications." After they are installed and you have logged into them, if you visit the Accounts & Sync settings as shown in the following sections, you see new accounts for each online service.

# Adding a Work Email Account

Your Galaxy Nexus can synchronize your contacts from your work email account as long as your company uses Microsoft Exchange or an email gateway that supports Microsoft ActiveSync (such as Lotus Traveler for Lotus Domino/Notes email systems). It might be useful to be able to keep your work and personal contacts on one mobile device instead of carrying two phones.

1. From the Home screen, pull down the Notification Bar.

2. Touch the Setting icon.

3. Touch Accounts & Sync.

4. Touch Add Account.

5. Touch Corporate.

6. Enter your full corporate email address.

7. Enter your corporate network password.

8. Touch Next.

9. Enter your company's mail server name.

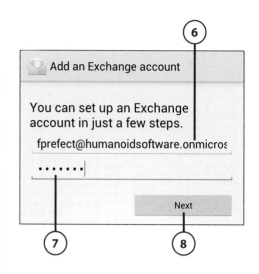

## Error Adding Account? Guess the Server

Your Galaxy Nexus tries to work out some information about your company's ActiveSync setup. If it can't, you are prompted to enter the ActiveSync server name manually. If you don't know what it is, you can try guessing it. If, for example, your email address is dsimons@allhitradio.com, the ActiveSync server is most probably webmail.allhitradio.com. If this doesn't work, ask your email administrator.

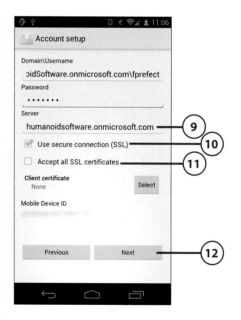

10. Touch to use secure connections, which encrypts your email, calendar, and contacts between your Galaxy Nexus and your company's mail server. It is highly recommended that you leave this selected.

11. Touch to accept all encryption certificates without validating them. It is not advisable to check this box because you could become the victim of hacking.

12. Touch Next.

**13.** Touch to agree that your mail administrator might impose security restrictions on your Galaxy Nexus if you proceed.

**14.** Touch to choose how often your corporate email is delivered to your Galaxy Nexus. Automatic means that as it arrives in your Inbox at work, it is delivered to your phone. You can set it to Manual, which means that your work email is only delivered when you open the Email app on your phone. You can also set the delivery frequency from every 5 minutes to every hour.

**15.** Touch to choose how many days in the past email is synchronized to your Galaxy Nexus or set it to All to synchronize all email in your Inbox.

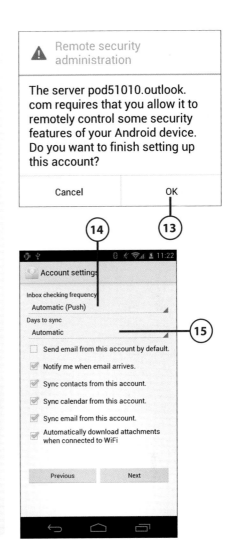

# Remote Security Administration

Remote Security Administration is another way of saying that when you activate your Galaxy Nexus against your work email servers, your email administrator can add restrictions to your phone. These can include forcing a device password, imposing the need for a very strong password, and requiring how many letters and numbers the password must be. It also means that your email administrator has the power to remotely wipe your Galaxy Nexus so that it is put back to factory defaults. This is normally done if you loose your phone or it is stolen.

**16.** Touch to enable or disable sending email from your Galaxy Nexus using your corporate email account by default. When enabled, any time you choose to compose a new email, your corporate account is used.

**17.** Touch to enable or disable being notified when new email arrives from your corporate Inbox.

**18.** Touch to enable or disable synchronizing your corporate contacts to your Galaxy Nexus.

**19.** Touch to enable or disable synchronizing your corporate calendar to your Galaxy Nexus.

**20.** Touch to enable or disable synchronizing your corporate email to your Galaxy Nexus.

**21.** Touch to enable or disable automatically downloading email attachments when your Galaxy Nexus is connected to a Wi-Fi network.

**22.** Touch Next.

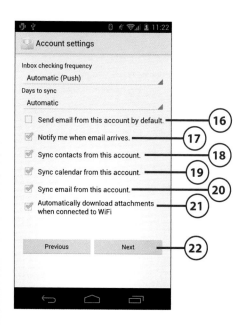

## What to Synchronize

You might decide that you don't want to synchronize all your work information to your Galaxy Nexus. You might decide to just synchronize email, and not the calendar, or maybe just the calendar but not the contacts and email. Unchecking these boxes enables you to choose the information you don't want to synchronize.

23. Touch Activate.

24. Enter a name for this email account. Use something meaningful that describes the purpose of the account such as "Work Email."

25. Touch Next to complete the setup.

## Remove an Account

To remove an account, from the Accounts & Sync screen, touch the account to be removed. Touch the Menu button on the top right of the screen and touch Remove Account.

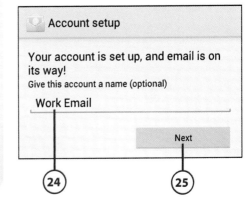

# Navigating People

The People app actually has three screens. The middle one you see shows you your list of contacts, but there are two others that have specific functions.

1. From the Home screen, touch the People icon.

2. Touch to add a new contact.

3. Touch to search for a contact.

4. Touch the Menu button to change the settings for the People app, manage accounts, import or export contacts, and choose which contacts to display.

5. Touch a contact to see all information about him.

6. Touch to see favorite contacts. This view also shows people you frequently contact.

7. Touch to see all contacts.

8. Touch to see contact groups. See more information about creating contact groups in the later section titled "Creating Contact Groups."

9. Touch a contact picture to see the Quick Connect Bar.

## Mark a Contact As Favorite

To mark a contact as a favorite, while you have the contact's information open, touch the star icon at the top of the screen.

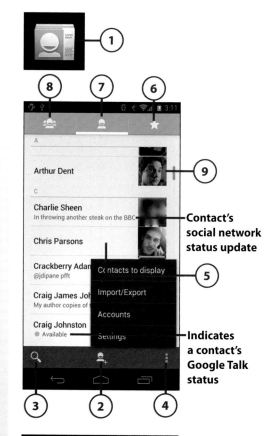

Contact's social network status update

Indicates a contact's Google Talk status

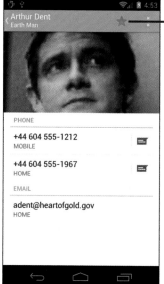

Mark a contact as a favorite

## Quick Connect Bar

When you touch a contact picture the Quick Connect Bar is displayed. This bar enables you to quickly access different ways of communicating with the contact.

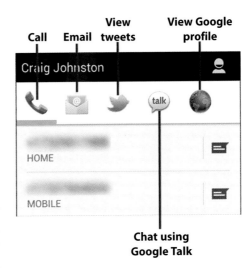

**Call**    **Email**    **View tweets**    **View Google profile**

**Chat using Google Talk**

# Checking a Contact's Status

If you have added contacts that belong to social networks such as Facebook, you can check their statuses right from the Contacts app.

1. Touch a contact.

2. Touch to view the contact's Twitter profile.

3. Swipe to the right to see the contact's social networking status updates.

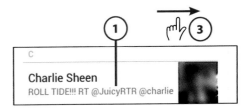

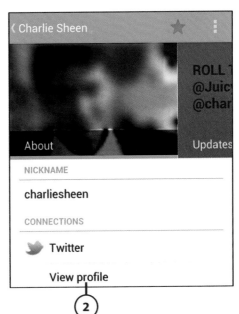

# Editing a Contact

Sometimes you need to make changes to a contact or add additional information to it.

1. Touch the contact to edit.

2. Press the Menu button.

3. Touch Edit.

4. Touch to enter a middle name, name prefix and suffix, and phonetic names.

5. Touch an X next to a field to delete it.

6. Touch to change the field subcategory. In this example, touching Mobile enables you to change the subcategory from Mobile to Home.

7. Touch Add New to add a new field in a specific category. In this example, touching Add New enables you to add a new phone number.

8. Scroll down for more contact information.

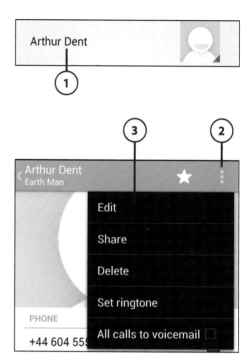

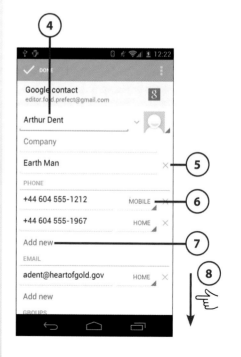

9. Touch to put the contact in a contact group. Contact groups can be family, friends, co-workers, or a group you create.

10. Touch to add a new field to the contact's contact card. New fields could be IM (Instant Messaging), Notes, Nickname, website, and even an Internet phone contact.

11. Touch Done to save your changes.

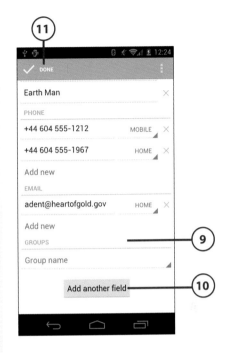

# Adding a Contact Photo

The contact photo is normally added automatically when a social network account is linked to a contact. However, you can manually add a picture.

1. Touch the Contact.

2. Touch the Menu button.

3. Touch Edit.

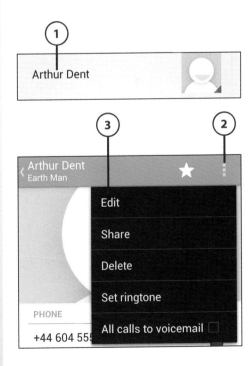

4. Touch the contact photo place-holder.

5. Touch to add a photo already saved on your Galaxy Nexus.

6. Touch the album where the photo is located.

7. Touch the photo.

**Take a photo with your camera instead**

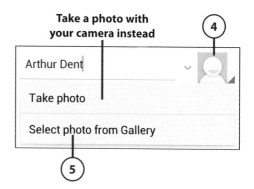

**Arthur Dent**

Take photo

Select photo from Gallery

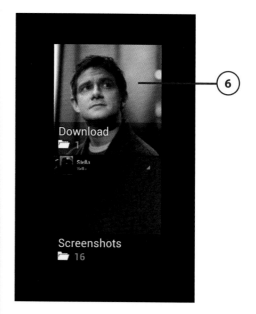

Download
1

Stella
Yell...

Screenshots
16

8. Drag the cropping box to select the area of the photo you want to use as the contact photo.

9. Drag the outside of the cropping box to expand or contract it.

10. Touch OK to save the cropped photo as the contact photo.

11. Touch Done to save the changes to the contact card.

## It's Not All Good

### Pixelated Contact Photos

If you allow your contacts to be synchronized from online sources such as Facebook, Twitter, or Google, for some reason the image quality of the photos look terrible when they arrive on your Galaxy Nexus. Right now there is nothing you can do to rectify this so the hope is that Google fixes this on its end because the contact photos synchronize via the Google servers.

# Adding and Managing Contacts

As you add contacts to your work email account or Google account, those contacts are synchronized to your Galaxy Nexus automatically. When you reply to or forward emails on your Galaxy Nexus to an email address that is not in your Contacts, those email addresses are automatically added to the contact list or merged into an existing contact with the same name. You can also add contacts to your Galaxy Nexus directly.

## Adding Contacts from an Email

To manually add a contact from an email, first open the email client (either email or Gmail) and then open an email. Please see Chapter 5, "Emailing," for more on how to work with email.

1.  Touch the blank contact picture to the left of the sender's name.

2.  Touch OK to add the sender's email address to your contacts.

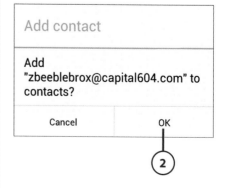

# Adding a Contact Manually

1. Touch the People icon on the Home screen.

2. Touch to add a new contact.

3. Touch to select which account the new contact is being added to. For example you might want to add the new contact to your work email account instead of your personal account.

4. Enter the person's full name including any middle name. Your Galaxy Nexus will automatically populate the first name, middle name, and last name fields.

5. Touch to choose a contact picture.

6. Scroll down to see more items to enter.

7. Touch Done to save the new contact.

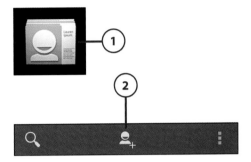

# Adding a Contact from a VCard

VCards are files that can be attached to emails. These VCards contain a virtual business card that you can import into the People app as a new contact. Use the following steps to save a VCard to your Galaxy Nexus.

1. Touch View under the attachment that has the .vcf extension.

2. Touch to select which account you want to add the new contact to. For example you might want to add the new contact to your work email account instead of your personal account.

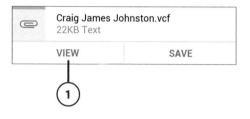

Craig James Johnston.vcf
22KB Text

VIEW      SAVE

Create contact under account

editor.ford.prefect@gmail.com
Google

fprefect@humanoidsoftware.
onmicrosoft.com
Corporate

# Adding a Contact Using Near Field Communications

Your Galaxy Nexus has Near Field Communications (NFC) functionality built in. This enables you to exchange contact cards between NFC-enabled smartphones or to purchase items in a store by just holding your Galaxy Nexus near the NFC reader at the check-out counter. If you encounter someone who has an NFC-enabled smartphone, or she has an NFC tag that contains her business card, follow these steps to import that information.

1. Hold the other person's smartphone back to back with your Galaxy Nexus, or hold the NFC tag close to the back cover of your Galaxy Nexus. Your Galaxy Nexus screen dims, and the phone plays a tone to indicate that it is reading the NFC information.

2. Touch to select which account you want to add the new contact to. For example you might want to add the new contact to your work email account instead of your personal account.

Create contact under account

**editor.ford.prefect@gmail.com**
Google

**fprefect@humanoidsoftware.onmicrosoft.com**
Corporate

2

## More About NFC

Your Galaxy Nexus has NFC built-in and the battery has an integrated antenna for NFC. When you hold another smartphone with NFC or an NFC tag close to the back cover, the antenna on the battery reads the data. See more about your Galaxy Nexus NFC antenna at http://www.ifixit.com/Teardown/Samsung-Galaxy-Nexus-Teardown/7182/1, and read more about NFC at http://en.wikipedia.org/wiki/Near_field_communication .

# People Settings

There are a couple of settings that you might want to customize for the People app, such as choosing the contact list display order and whether to display contacts using their first names first or last names first.

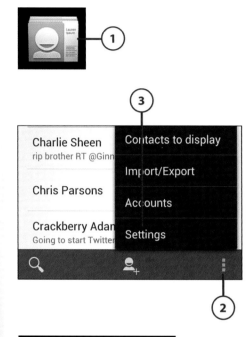

1. Touch the People icon on the Home screen.

2. Touch the Menu button.

3. Touch Settings.

4. Touch to choose the sort order of the list of contacts in the People app. You can sort the list by first name or last name.

5. Touch to choose how each contact is displayed. You can display contacts as first name first or last name first.

6. Touch Back to save the settings.

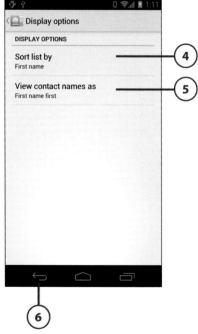

# Creating Contact Groups

You can create contact groups—such as Friends, Family, Inner Circle—and then divide your contacts among them. This can be useful if you don't want to search through all your contacts to find a family member. Instead you can just touch the Family group and see only family members.

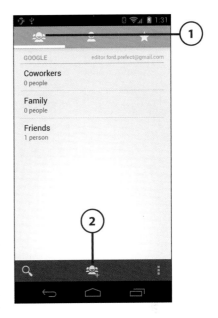

1. Touch the Groups icon from the People main screen.

2. Touch the New Group icon.

3. Touch the account where you want to create the new group.

4. Enter a name for your new group.

5. Start typing the name of a contact to add to the group. Your Galaxy Nexus will display names that match what you are typing.

6. Touch the name from the list of matches to add that person to the new group.

7. Repeat steps 5 and 6 to add more people to the group.

8. Touch Done to save the group.

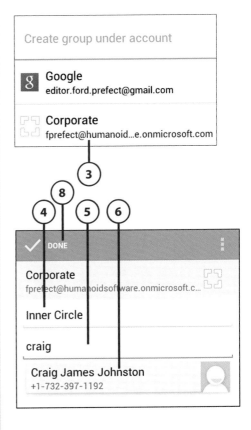

# Editing Contact Groups

1. Touch the Groups icon from the People main screen.

2. Touch the group to edit.

3. Touch the Menu button.

4. Touch Edit.

5. Touch to change the name of the group. Note that some Google groups cannot be renamed.

6. Enter a name to add an extra person to the group.

7. Touch the X icon next to a contact to remove them from the group.

8. Touch Done to save the group.

# Choosing Contacts To Display

You can choose to hide certain contact groups from the main contacts display. For example, show only contacts from Twitter. You can also choose which contact groups in each account to include.

1. Touch the People icon on the Home screen.

2. Touch the Menu button.

3. Touch Contacts to Display.

4. Touch to show all contacts from all accounts.

5. Touch an account to show only contacts in that account.

6. Touch to customize which groups in each account are displayed.

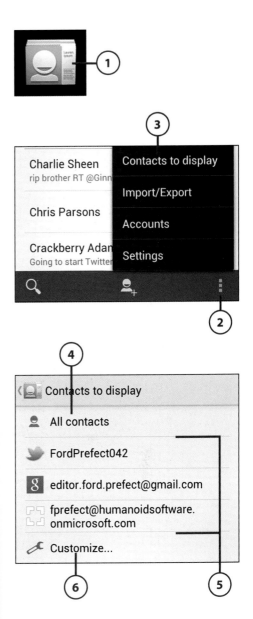

7. Touch to expand an account to see subgroups of contacts.

8. Touch to select or deselect a subgroup of contacts.

9. Touch OK to save the settings.

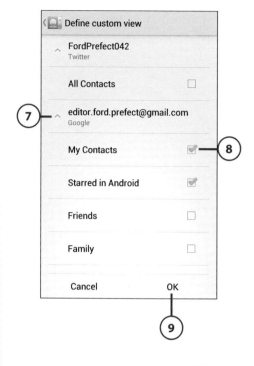

# Joining and Separating Contacts

As you add contacts to your Galaxy Nexus, they are automatically merged if the new contact name matches a name that's already stored. Sometimes you need to manually join contacts together or separate them if your Galaxy Nexus has joined them in error.

## Joining Contacts Manually

1. Touch the contact you want to join a contact to.

2. Touch the Menu button.

3. Touch Edit.

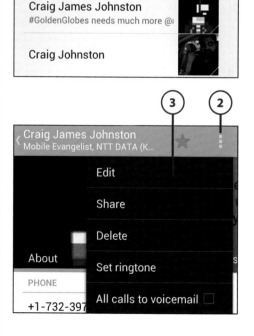

4. Touch the Menu button.

5. Touch Join.

6. Touch the contact you want to join with.

7. Touch Done to complete the join process.

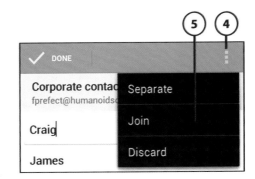

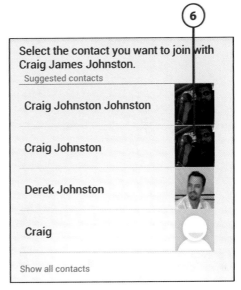

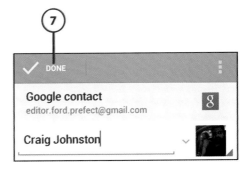

## Separating Contacts

1. Touch the contact you want to separate.

2. Touch the Menu button.

3. Touch Edit.

4. Touch the Menu button.

5. Touch Separate.

6. Touch OK to separate the contacts.

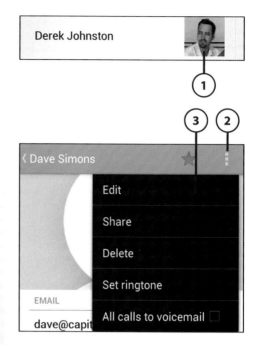

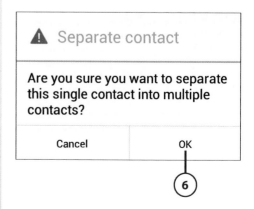

# Adding a Contact to Your Home Screen

If you communicate with some contacts so much that you are constantly opening and closing the People application, a quicker solution might be to add a shortcut to the contacts on the Home screen.

1. Touch the Launcher icon.

2. Touch Widgets.

3. Swipe right until you see the Contact widget.

4. Touch and hold the Contact widget.

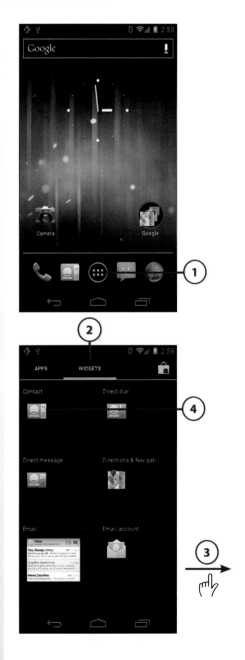

5. While still holding the widget, position the widget on the Home screen and release your finger.

6. Touch the contact you want to add to the Home screen.

# IMPORTING AND EXPORTING CONTACTS

>>>Go Further

You can import any contacts that are stored on your SIM card (GSM Galaxy Nexus only) or VCards that you have saved to your Galaxy Nexus internal storage. You can also export your entire contact list to your Galaxy Nexus internal storage or share that entire contact list via Bluetooth, email, Gmail, or, if you have any NFC tag writer software installed, write it to an NFC tag. To access the import/export functions, touch the Menu button and touch Import/Export.

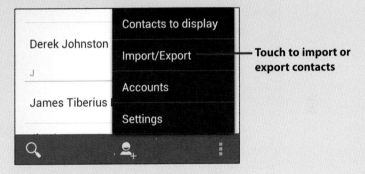

**Touch to import or export contacts**

Make and
receive calls

In this chapter, you learn about your Galaxy Nexus Phone application. You learn how to place and receive calls, manage them, and use Google Voice as your voicemail. Topics include the following:

2

→ Placing and receiving calls
→ Managing in-progress calls
→ Conducting conference calls
→ Setting up Google Voice
→ Using Google Voice for voicemail

# Using the Phone and Google Voice

As with any good smartphone, your Galaxy Nexus has a great phone that allows for making and receiving calls, voicemail, three-way calling, and many other features. However, your Galaxy Nexus can also use Google Voice to save you money on calls and to transcribe your voicemail if you want it to. This chapter covers your Galaxy Nexus phone in detail and goes over how to set up and use Google Voice.

## Getting to Know the Phone Application

Let's take a look at the Phone app and learn its different features including how to do conference calling.

1. Touch the Phone icon on the Home screen. The phone application launches and displays the familiar phone keypad.

2. Type a phone number.

3. Touch the green phone icon to place the call.

4. Touch and hold the 1 key to listen to your voicemail.

5. Touch the delete icon to correct a phone number, or touch and hold the icon to remove the entire number.

6. Touch to search for a contact to call.

7. Touch to show the phone dialer tab.

8. Touch to show the call log.

9. Touch to see all of your contacts.

10. Touch the Menu button to change your Phone settings.

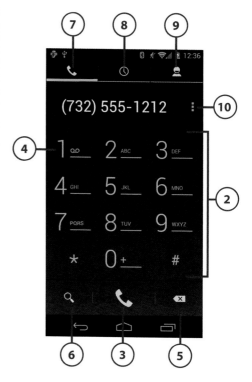

## PAUSES AND WAITS

To add a two-second pause (symbolized by a ",") or a wait (symbolized by a ";") into your phone number, touch the Menu button, and touch the appropriate item. When you touch Add Wait, your Galaxy Nexus dials the number up to the point of the wait and then waits until it hears a response from the other side. You can insert multiple two-second pauses if you need to. Pauses and waits can be useful when using calling cards, doing phone banking, or dialing into conference calls.

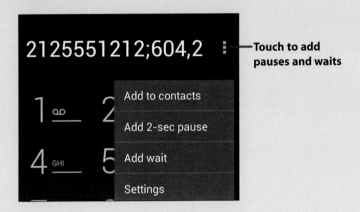

Touch to add pauses and waits

### International Numbers

Normally when you dial international numbers, you have to use some kind of code before the country code (such as 011 in the U.S. or 00 in other countries). With your Galaxy Nexus, you don't need to know that special code; just type a plus sign, then the country code, then the rest of the number, dropping any zeros before the area code. This is useful when you travel outside your home country because you don't need to know the dialing code. For example, 011 44 604 555-1212 becomes +44 604 555-1212.

Touch and hold to add a +

# Call Log

The Call Log tab shows the history of all incoming, outgoing, and missed calls.

1. Touch the Call Log tab.

2. Touch to see more information about the call.

3. Touch to call the person back.

4. Touch to search your call history.

5. Touch the Menu button and Clear call log to clear the call log.

# Contacts

The Contacts tab shows your frequently called contacts and all contacts for whom you have stored phone numbers.

1. Touch the Contacts tab.

2. Frequently called contacts are displayed here.

3. Scroll down to see all contacts who have phone numbers.

4. Touch to search your contacts.

5. Touch the Menu button to change the Phone settings, add a new contact, and change which contacts are displayed.

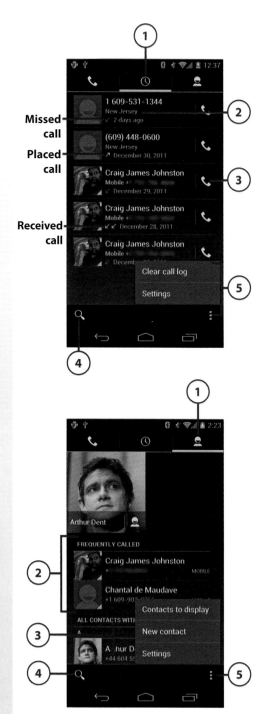

Missed call

Placed call

Received call

# Phone Settings

You can change many aspects of how the Phone works on your Galaxy Nexus including voicemail, call forwarding, and caller ID.

1. Touch the Menu button. Please note that on the Call Log and Contacts tabs, the Menu button is on the bottom right of the screen.

2. Touch Settings.

3. Touch to set and manage Fixed Dialing Numbers.

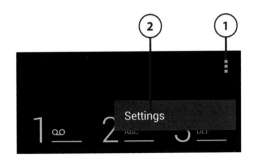

## What Is Fixed Number Dialing (FDN for short)?

Fixed Number Dialing is a feature that allows you to set a fixed list of phone numbers that can be dialed from your phone. This could be useful as a way to limit a child's use the Galaxy Nexus or limit usage if you lend your Galaxy Nexus to someone. You can enable FDN and set a PIN so that the list of numbers can't be changed unless your PIN is re-entered.

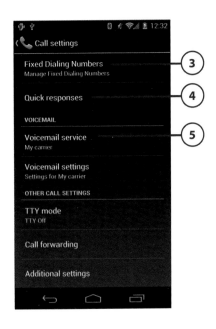

4. Touch to edit your Quick Reponses.

## What Are Quick Responses?

When someone calls you, you can send him or her a short text message (SMS) instead of answering the call. You edit the text messages using this setting selection. When a call comes in, you can simply choose which one to send. Please see the "Receiving an Incoming Call" section later in this chapter to see how to use Quick Responses.

5. Touch to choose your voicemail service.

## Why Would You Use a Different VoiceMail Service?

You might want to take advantage of a voicemail service that provides extra features such as voicemail transcription, or you might choose to direct all incoming missed calls to a single voicemail box to reduce the need to call multiple voicemail boxes. You might also want to take advantage of Google Voice and its voicemail features. Read more about Google Voice later in this chapter.

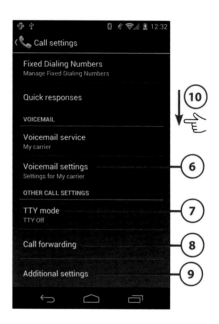

6. Touch to change the phone number of your Voicemail service.

7. Touch to enable TTY and choose the TTY Mode. You can choose TTY Full, TTY HCO, or TTY VCO.

8. Touch to change your Call Forwarding options. You must have cellular coverage to view or change these settings because they are stored at your wireless carrier.

9. Touch to change your Caller ID and Call Waiting settings. You must have cellular coverage to view or change these settings because they are stored at your wireless carrier.

10. Scroll down for more settings.

11. Touch to add and manage Internet Call (also known as Session Initiation Protocol or SIP) accounts.

12. Touch to choose when to use Internet Calling. You can choose to use it for all calls when a data network is available, for Internet-based calls only, or ask each time you place a call.

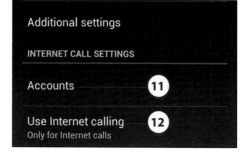

# Fixed Dialing Numbers (GSM only)

Fixed Dialing Numbers (FDN) is used to restrict your Galaxy Nexus (or any GSM-compliant phone) to be able to dial only a specific list of phone numbers. To enable this feature you must ask your wireless carrier for the PIN2 code. This is a second lock code for your SIM card and is separate from the PIN1, which is the lock PIN you set.

1.  Touch Fixed Dialing Numbers from the Phone Settings screen.

2.  Touch to enable FDN. Remember you must already have your SIM card's PIN2 code from your wireless carrier.

3.  Touch to change the PIN2 code.

4.  Touch to manage the list of numbers on the FDN.

5.  Touch the Menu button.

6.  Touch Add Contact.

7.  Enter a contact name.

8.  Enter a contact phone number.

9.  Touch the Menu button to import contact from the People app.

10. Touch to import contacts from the People app.

11. Touch to save the contact.

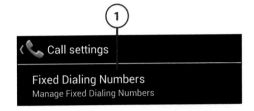

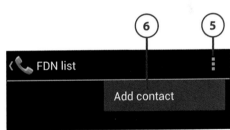

# Quick Responses

Quick Responses are text messages (SMS) that you can choose to send to an incoming caller instead of answering the call or sending it to voicemail. You can only store four Quick Responses, but you can edit them.

1. Touch Quick Responses from the Phone Settings screen.

2. Touch one of the four Quick Responses to edit it.

3. Edit the Quick Response text.

4. Touch OK to save the changes.

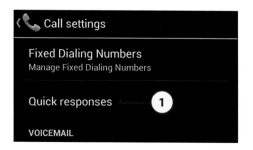

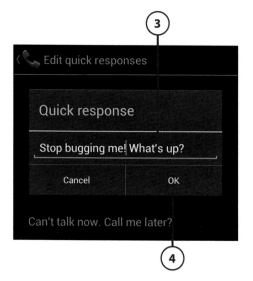

# Call Forwarding

Call forwarding is normally used to send calls to voicemail when you don't answer or you are unavailable, however it can be used to forward all calls to a new phone number, or select what numbers calls are forwarded to based on circumstances.

1. Touch Call Forwarding from the Phone Settings screen.

2. Touch to enable or disable forwarding all incoming calls to a specific phone number or edit the number the calls are being forwarded to.

3. Touch to enable or disable forwarding incoming calls to a specific phone number when you are already on a call (busy), or edit the number the calls are being forwarded to.

4. Touch to enable or disable forwarding incoming calls to a specific phone number when you don't answer the call, or edit the number the calls are being forwarded to.

5. Touch to enable or disable forwarding incoming calls to a specific phone number when you are unreachable (out of coverage or your phone is off), or edit the number the calls are being forwarded to.

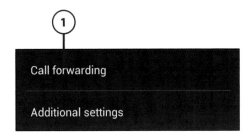

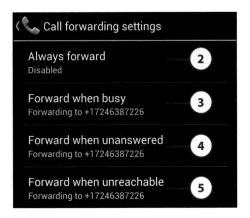

# Internet Calling (SIP)

Your Galaxy Nexus has the built-in
ability to make and receive Internet
calls. Internet calls use Voice over IP
(VoIP) technology to digitize calls
and send them over the Internet as
opposed to using your wireless carrier's voice network. Here is how to set
up Internet calling. You must already
have signed up with an SIP provider
and have written down the settings
you need to use for the setup.

1. Touch Accounts from the Phone
   Settings screen.

2. Touch to enable or disable the
   ability to receive Internet calls
   (SIP calls) on your Galaxy Nexus.
   Please remember that enabling
   your phone to receive calls reduc-
   es your battery life.

3. Touch to add an Internet Calling
   (SIP) account.

4. Enter the username for your SIP account.

5. Enter the password for your SIP account.

6. Touch to enter the servername for your SIP account. You should have received this from your SIP provider.

7. Touch to enable or disable using this SIP account as the default SIP account when making Internet calls.

8. Touch to enter optional information such as a proxy servername.

9. Touch the Menu button.

10. Touch Save.

11. Touch to return to the main Settings screen.

12. Touch to choose when to use Internet calling. You can choose For All Calls when a data network is available, Only for Internet Calls, which is when a contact you are calling actually has an SIP address, or Ask for Each Call to be prompted every time you place a call.

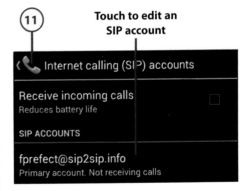

**Touch to edit an SIP account**

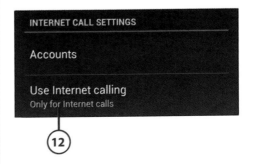

# Receiving a Call

When you receive a call, you have three choices for handling it.

1. Slide the phone icon to the right to answer the call.

2. Slide the phone icon to the left to send the call to voicemail.

3. Slide the phone icon up to send a Quick Response (SMS) to the caller.

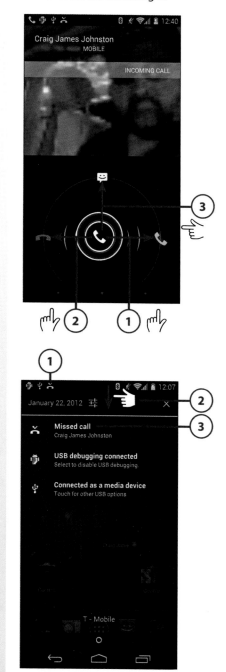

## Handling Missed Calls

1. If you miss a call, the missed call icon displays in the Notification Bar.

2. Pull down the Notification Bar to see how many calls you've missed.

3. Touch the missed calls notification to open your Galaxy Nexus Call Log.

# Placing a Call

You can place calls on your Galaxy Nexus in a few ways. You can manually dial a number into the Phone application, touch a phone number in a contact entry, command your Galaxy Nexus using your voice, or touch a phone number on a web page, in an email, or in a calendar appointment.

## Dialing from a Contact Entry

1. Touch the People application on the Home screen.

2. Touch the name of the person you want to call.

3. Touch the phone number you want to call.

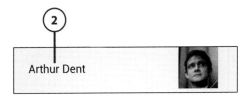

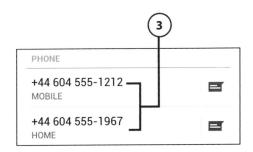

# Dialing Using Your Voice (Voice Dialer)

You can place calls using the Galaxy Nexus' built-in microphone or a Bluetooth headset by making use of the Voice Dialer app. This app is sometimes not very accurate, but it does support Bluetooth, which makes it good for dialing while you're driving.

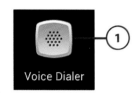

Voice Dialer

1. Touch Voice Dialer app icon in the Launcher.

2. When the Listening screen displays, say "Call" and the person's name. For example "Call Arthur Dent." Your Galaxy Nexus finds that person in your Contacts and displays the phone numbers on the screen. You can also speak numbers to dial.

3. Touch the phone number you'd like to call or say the number's label, for example "Home" or "Mobile."

## Be More Specific

If you know there are multiple phone numbers for a particular contact you want to call, you can be more specific when speaking your command to reduce the number of steps it takes to place the call. For example you can say "Call Arthur Dent Mobile" to dial Arthur Dent's mobile number immediately.

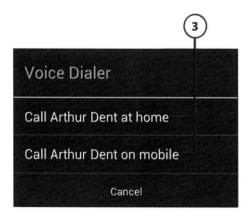

# Dialing Using Your Voice (Google Voice Search)

You can place calls using the Galaxy Nexus built-in microphone by making use of the Google Voice Search. This app is very accurate, but it does not support Bluetooth headsets.

1. Touch the microphone in the Google Search Widget.

2. Say "Call" and the person's name. For example "Call Arthur Dent." Your Galaxy Nexus finds that person in your Contacts and displays the phone numbers on the screen. You can also speak numbers to dial.

3. Touch the phone number you'd like to call.

# Options While on a Call

While on a phone call, you can mute and unmute the call, switch the audio between your Galaxy Nexus and a Bluetooth headset, bring up the dial pad, and enable the speaker phone.

1. Touch the Dialpad icon to display the dialpad and type additional numbers during the call, for example for phone banking. While the dialpad is displayed, the Dialpad icon changes to the Hide Dialpad icon. Touch it to hide the dialpad.

2. Touch to switch the call audio between your Galaxy Nexus ear piece, your Galaxy Nexus speaker (for speaker phone), and a Bluetooth headset.

---

## Need to Know More About Bluetooth?

Read Chapter 4, "Connecting to the Internet, Bluetooth Devices, and VPNs," for help on setting up Bluetooth headsets.

---

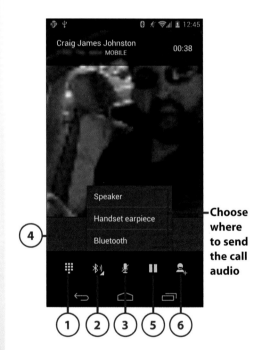

Choose where to send the call audio

3. Touch to mute your audio on the call.

4. Touch the red bar to end the call.

5. Touch to put the call on hold.

6. Touch to add someone to the call and start a conference call.

# Conference Calling

While on a call, you can create an impromptu conference call by adding callers.

1. Touch the Add Call icon. Your current call goes on hold.

2. A second dialpad appears. Either type in the number for the person to call, or touch the Contacts icon to dial from your contacts. When the second call connects, a screen opens for you to merge the calls.

3. Touch Merge to join the two calls together into one conference call.

## Adding Multiple Callers

While on the conference call touch the Add Call icon again to add another caller. The number of callers you can add to a conference call depends on what your wireless carrier supports.

**Dial from Contacts**

**Type a new number**

# Managing a Conference Call

While on a conference call, you can add more callers or split callers off from the conference call.

1. Touch to add another caller to the conference call.

2. Touch to end the entire conference call.

3. Touch to manage the conference call.

4. Touch to hangup and remove a caller from the conference call.

5. Touch to remove a caller from the conference call but keep the person on hold.

6. Touch to return to the conference call.

## Work While on a Call

While you are on a call, you can switch away from the Phone app and work in any app on your Galaxy Nexus. An icon in the Notification Bar indicates that you are still in a call. To switch back to the Phone app, pull down the Notification Bar and touch the call in progress.

Active call icon

Touch the active call to return to the Phone app

# Dial from a Web Page or Other App

Your Galaxy Nexus is always on the lookout for phone numbers on web pages, in email, and in text messages. You can select these phone numbers to dial them.

1. Touch and hold on a phone number. You might need to zoom in on the number first if you are on a website.

2. Touch Dial to place the call.

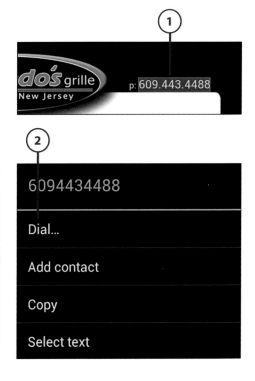

## Sound Settings

You can adjust sound settings for the Phone app by adjusting the volume, setting ringtones, and turning on or off the dialpad tones.

1. From the Home screen, pull down the Notification Bar.

2. Touch the Settings icon.

**3.** Touch Sound.

**4.** Touch to adjust the ringtone volume for incoming calls.

**5.** Touch to select the default ringtone to use for incoming calls. This ringtone plays unless you have set a specific custom ringtone for a particular contact.

**6.** Touch to change the default notification sound that plays when a new notification is displayed in the status bar, like a missed call.

**7.** Touch to enable or disable audible touch tones when you press numbers on the dialpad.

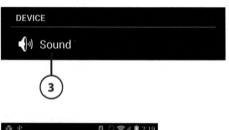

# Google Voice

Regular Google Voice, if set up on your Galaxy Nexus, enables you to save money on international calls and have your voicemails transcribed into text. If you upgrade Google Voice, which is free, you have some extra features, such as choosing your own personalized phone number or setting up simultaneous ringing.

# Setting Up Google Voice

If you want to start using the Google Voice features on your Galaxy Nexus, you need to do some setup. If you do not have Google Voice installed, download it from the AnGalaxy Nexus Market. See Chapter 10, "Working with Android Applications," for more on how to use the AnGalaxy Nexus Market.

1. Touch the Voice icon on the Home screen.

2. Read the welcome information from Google Voice and touch Next.

3. Select the account to use for Google Voice if you synchronize to multiple Google Accounts.

4. Touch Sign In to proceed.

5. Touch Allow Access.

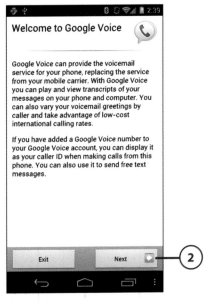

Use a different Google account

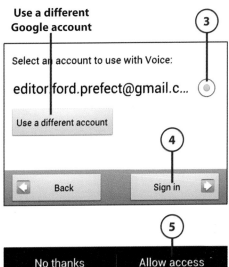

6. Touch Next.

7. Touch Add This Phone.

8. Touch Next to verify your phone number automatically.

9. Touch Next after your number has been verified.

10. Select how you want to use Google Voice.

11. Touch Next to allow Google to access your setting so you can set up your voicemail.

12. Touch Next.

13. Touch Configure to set up Google Voice as the voicemail provider for your phone. Touch Skip if you don't want to do this.

14. Touch Google Voice.

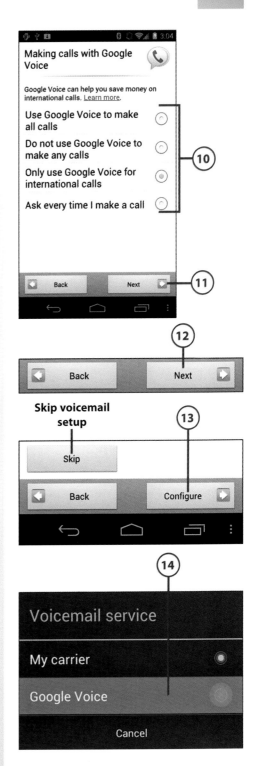

**15.** Touch OK.

**16.** Touch Finish.

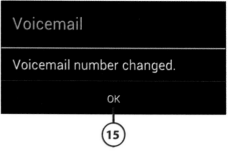

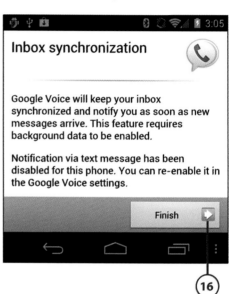

## Upgrading Google Voice

If you want to use the advanced features of Google Voice, you need to upgrade your account. You can upgrade free of charge. To upgrade, use your desktop computer to go to http://google.com/voice and log in using your Google account.

**1.** Click the cog icon and choose Voice Settings.

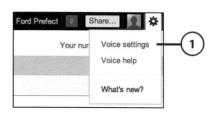

2. Click Get a Google Number.

3. Click Continue.

4. Type search criteria in the box to search for available Google Voice phone numbers, including numbers that spell words.

5. Select a number from the options.

6. Click Continue.

7. Click Continue on the Confirm Your Number screen.

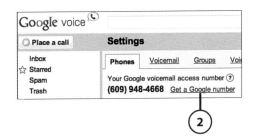

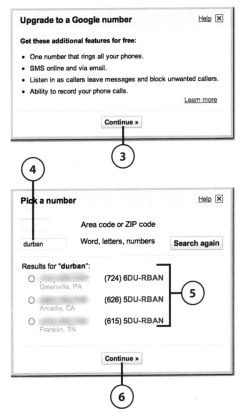

**8.** Enable call forwarding from your current mobile number to your new Google Voice number by following the instructions on the screen and touching Done.

### It Might Cost You

Please be aware that some wireless carriers charge to forward calls, many times on a per-forwarded-call basis, so check with your carrier before enabling the option to forward calls.

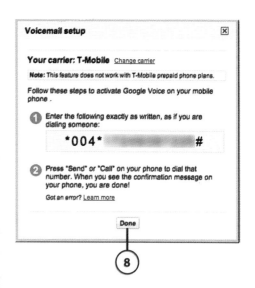

# Playing Back and Managing Google Voicemails

New Google voicemails are delivered to your Google Voice Inbox. Launch Google Voice and follow these steps to play back and manage your voicemails.

**1.** Touch a new voicemail to read it or play back the audio.

**2.** Touch the play icon to play the message audio.

### Sometimes Google Guesses

Grayed-out words in a voicemail transcript are words that Google Voice is unsure of.

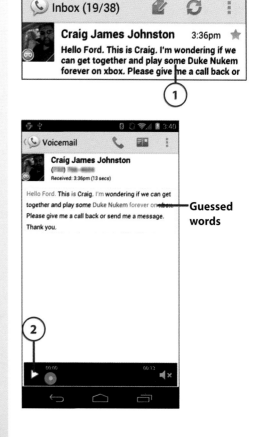

Guessed words

3. Touch to call the person who left the voicemail.

4. Touch to send a text message to the person who left the voicemail.

5. Touch the Menu button to see actions you can take on the voicemail.

6. Touch to archive the voicemail.

7. Touch to mark the person who left the voicemail as one of your favorite contacts.

8. Touch to delete the voicemail.

# Google Voice Settings

After you have been using Google Voice for a while, you may want to change some of the settings.

1. Touch the Menu button.

2. Touch Settings.

3. Touch to enable or disable Do Not Disturb. Enabling this setting sends all incoming calls to voice-mail.

4. Touch to change how you use Google Voice.

5. Touch to choose where Google Voice voicemails are played back. Your choices are speakphone or handset earpiece.

6. Touch to sign out of Google Voice.

7. Touch to configure Google Voice synchronization and notification settings.

## Google Voice Sync and Notifications

After you have been using Google Voice for a while, you might want to change some of the settings.

1. Touch to change how the background data for your Galaxy Nexus synchronization is handled.

2. Touch to choose which apps handle SMS (text messages). You can have both the Messages app and Google Voice handle them, or just Google Voice.

3. Touch to enable and disable text message notifications for text messages received only in your Google Voice inbox.

4. Touch to enable or disable notifications when you receive a new Google Voice message.

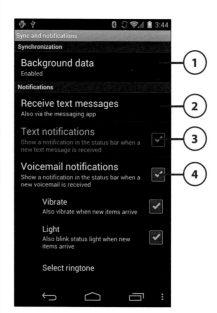

5.  Touch to enable or disable vibration along with Google Voice inbox notifications.

6.  Touch to enable or disable blinking of the notification light when you receive a new item in your Google Voice inbox.

7.  Touch to choose a ringtone when a new item arrives in your Google Voice inbox.

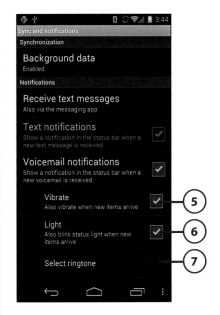

Search for and
purchase music

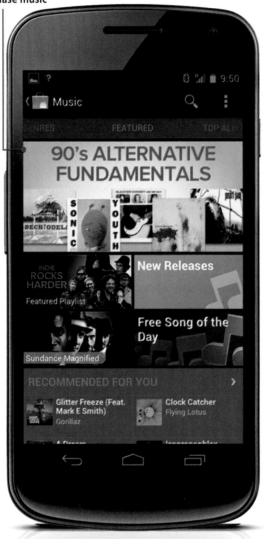

In this chapter, you learn about Galaxy Nexus audio and video capabilities, including how your Galaxy Nexus plays video and music, and how you can synchronize audio and video from your desktop computer or Google Music. This chapter also covers how to take pictures and video. Topics include the following:

→ Using Google Music for music

→ The Gallery application for pictures and video

→ Video effects

→ YouTube

# Audio, Video, and Books

Your Galaxy Nexus is a strong multimedia smartphone with the ability to play back many different audio and video formats. The large screen enables you to turn your Galaxy Nexus sideways to enjoy a video in its original 16:9 ratio. You can also use your Galaxy Nexus to search YouTube, watch videos, and even upload videos to YouTube right from your phone. Android version 4 fully embraces the cloud, which enables you to store your music collection on Google's servers so you can access it anywhere.

## The Music Application

Your Galaxy Nexus ships with an app called Google Music, which enables you to listen to music stored on your phone as well as from your collection in the Google Music cloud.

# Updating the Music Application

Your Galaxy Nexus ships with an older, beta version of Google Music rather than the most recent version. You should upgrade it to the latest version.

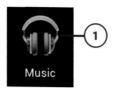

Music

1. Touch the Music icon.

2. Touch the Menu button.

3. Touch Settings.

4. Touch Google Account.

5. Select your Google account. This is also known as your Gmail account.

6. Touch to exit and save your settings.

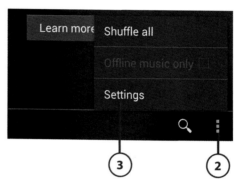

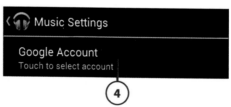

7. Touch the Android Market icon.

8. Touch to check the box.

9. Touch Market.

10. Touch the Menu button.

11. Touch My Music.

12. Touch OK.

13. Touch Update.

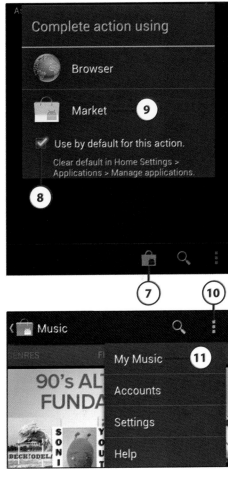

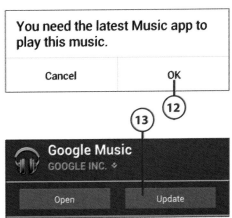

14.  Touch Accept & Download.

15.  Touch Open.

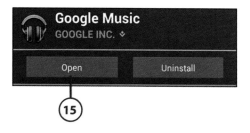

# Finding Music

Now that the Google Music app is up to date, you can add some music. One way to add music is to purchase it from Google.

1.  Touch the Music icon on the Home screen if the Music app isn't already running.

2.  Touch the Market icon.

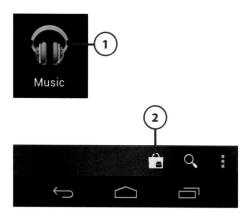

3. Touch to see new releases.

4. Touch to see staff picks.

5. Touch to see what music is recommended for you based on previous purchases.

6. Swipe left to see a list of music Genres.

7. Swipe right to see the Top Albums and Top Songs.

8. Touch to search for music.

# Purchasing Music

After you find a song or album you want to purchase, follow these steps.

## Free Music

Sometimes songs are offered for free. If a song is offered for free, you see the word FREE instead of a price for the song. Even though the song is free, you still need to follow the steps outlined in this section; however, the price is reflected as 0.

1. Touch the price to the right of the song title or album.

**Touch to play a preview of the song before purchasing it**

2. Touch Accept & Buy.

3. Touch Listen to hear your song after the purchase is complete. You can also play the song or album from within the Music app.

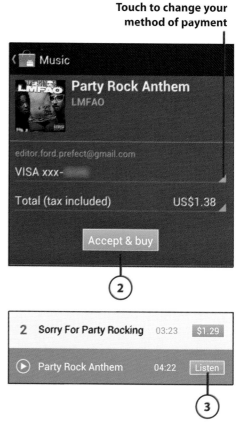

**Touch to change your method of payment**

## It's Not All Good

**Cloud and Data Usage**

Although the idea of cloud storage (where your music is stored on Google computers as opposed to your Galaxy Nexus) is very beneficial, it does mean that anytime you listen to your music collection, it is streamed over the network. If you are connected to Wi-Fi then this data streaming is free; however, if you are not connected to Wi-Fi the data is streamed over the cellular network and counts against your data package. If you don't have a large or unlimited data package, your could incur large overage fees, so please be careful. Another disadvantage of streaming from the Cloud is that when you have no cellular or Wi-Fi coverage, or you have very slow or spotty coverage you are unable to access and listen to your music collection, or the songs stutter because of the poor connection. Be extra careful about this when travelling abroad because international data roaming charges are very expensive.

# Adding Your Existing Music to Google Music

You can upload up to 20,000 songs from Apple iTunes, Microsoft Windows Media Player, or music stored in folders on your computer for free to your Google Music cloud account by using the Google Music Manager app on your desktop computer. If you haven't already installed Google Music Manager, please follow the steps in "Installing Google Music Manager" section in the "Prologue."

1. Click (right-click for Windows) on the Google Music Manager icon. (This icon is in the Mac Menu Bar at the top of the screen or in the Windows Task Bar at the bottom of the screen).

2. Choose Preferences. (Use the Options command if you are on Windows).

3. Click to upload new songs that have been added.

4. Click to upload the remainder of songs that have not yet uploaded.

5. Click to upload songs in certain playlists. This only works for iTunes or for Windows Media Player.

6. Choose the playlists to upload.

7. Click Upload after you have made your selections.

8. Click to allow Google Music Manager to automatically upload new songs added.

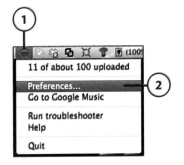

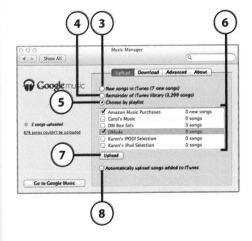

## Automatic Upload

If you choose to have your music uploaded automatically in step 8, Google Music Manager continually monitors Apple iTunes, Microsoft Windows Media Player, or your Music folders to see when you add music. If it finds new music, Google Music Manager automatically uploads it. (After you install Google Music Manager, the software is always running on your computer.)

## What If I Don't Have iTunes or Windows Media Player?

If you don't have or don't use Apple iTunes or Microsoft Windows Media Player to store and play your music, Google Music Manager can upload music from folders on your computer. Click the Advanced Tab, click Change, and select either Music folder (to use the folder on your computer called Music) or Other folders (so you can choose folders where you store your music). Click Add Folder to add a new folder to the list.

## Can I Download Music to My Computer?

You can download your entire music collection from Google Music to your computer, or just download music you have purchased on your Galaxy Nexus by clicking the Download tab in Google Music Manager Preferences.

# Using the Music Application

Now that you have some music synchronized to Google Music, it's time to take a look at the Google Music app on your Galaxy Nexus.

**1.** Touch the Music icon on the Home screen.

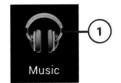

### Swipe Between Tabs

As you follow the steps in this task, instead of touching the heading tabs such as Albums and Artists, you can swipe left and right to move between these tabs instead.

2. Touch Artists to filter the view by artist. Touch an artist's name to reveal songs by that artist and then touch a song to play it.

3. Touch Albums to filter the view by album title. Touch an album name to reveal songs on that album and then touch a song to play it.

4. Touch Songs to filter the view by song title. This shows all songs by all artists. Touch a song to play it.

5. Touch Playlists to show any music playlists that you have synchronized to your Galaxy Nexus. Find out more about how to do that later in the chapter.

6. Touch Genres to filter the view by genre. Touch an album name to reveal songs on that album and then touch a song to play it.

7. Touch Recent to see recently played songs, mixes, or albums.

8. Touch to get music from the Market.

9. Touch to search for music in your collection.

What's currently playing

# Controlling Playback

While your music is playing, you have some control over how a song plays and the selection of music that plays.

1. Touch to jump to the previous song in the album, playlist, or shuffle.

2. Touch to jump to the next song in the album, playlist, or shuffle.

3. Touch to pause the song. The button turns into the play button when a song is paused. Touch again to resume playing a paused song.

4. Drag to skip forward and backward through the song.

5. Touch the up arrow or the album art to reveal more information about the song.

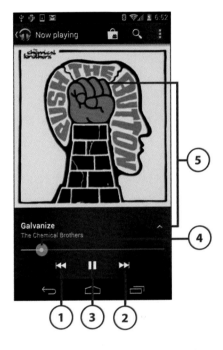

6. Touch to enable or disable song shuffling. When Shuffle is enabled, songs in the current playlist, album, or song list are randomly played.

7. Touch to enable repeating. Touch once to repeat all songs; touch again to repeat the current song only; touch again to disable repeating.

8. Touch to see all songs in the album. Only songs that you have purchased or downloaded are displayed.

9. Touch to see all songs by the artist. Only songs that you have purchased or downloaded are displayed.

10. Touch to add the song to an existing playlist or to create a new playlist using this song.

11. Touch to make an instant mix based on the song or shop for more songs by the artist.

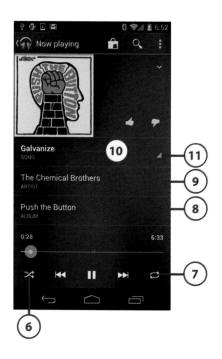

### What Is an Instant Mix?

If you are playing a song and choose to create an Instant Mix as mentioned in step 11, the Google Music app creates a new playlist and adds songs to it that are similar to the one you are currently playing. The name of the playlist is the name of the current song plus the word mix. For example if you are playing the song "Galvanize" and choose to create an Instant Mix, the playlist is called "Galvanize Mix."

**No repeating**

**Repeat all songs**

**Repeat current song**

12. Touch to indicate that you like the song. The Google Music app adds the song to the "Thumbs up" play-list.

13. Touch to indicate that you do not like the song.

14. Touch the Menu button to use the graphic equalizer to adjust the way the song sounds and adjust the settings for the Google Music app.

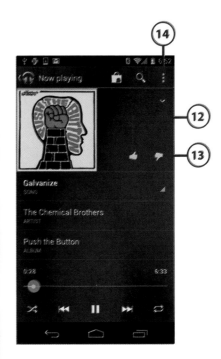

# Adjust the Equalizer

The Google Music app has a Graphic Equalizer that enables you to select preset audio configurations or use your own. While a song is playing, use the following steps to use or adjust the Equalizer.

1. Touch the Menu button.

2. Touch Sound Effects.

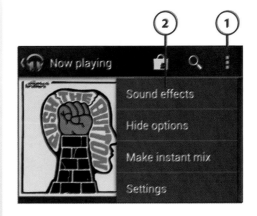

3. Touch to turn the Equalizer on and off.

4. Touch to select from a list of preset Equalizer settings such as Dance, Hip Hop, and many more.

5. Drag the frequency response sliders to enhance or deemphasize certain frequencies.

6. Drag the slider to adjust the bass boost.

7. Drag the slider to adjust the 3D effect, which helps the music sound like its all around as opposed to just in your two ears.

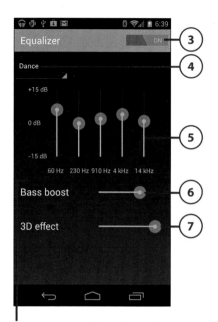

# Work and Listen to Music

You can only adjust these when you are using headphones

You don't have to keep the Google Music app open while you are playing music—you can switch back to the Home screen and run any other app but still have the ability to control the music.

1. Pull down the Notification Bar.

2. Touch to pause the song.

3. Touch to jump to the next song in the list, album, or playlist.

4. Touch the song title to open the Google Music app for more control.

5. Touch to stop playing the song and remove the playback control from the Notification Bar.

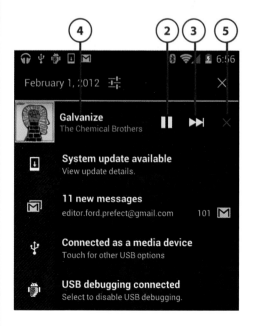

## What If I Get a Call?

If someone calls you while you are listening to music, your Galaxy Nexus pauses the music and displays the regular incoming call screen. After you hang up, the music continues playing.

# Managing Playlists

Playlists enable you to group songs together. Here is how to create them and use them.

## Creating a New Playlist on Your Galaxy Nexus

1. Touch the Playlists tab.

2. Touch the plus icon to create a new playlist.

3. Enter a name for your new playlist.

4. Touch OK.

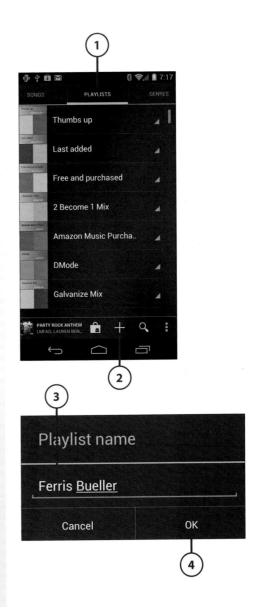

# Adding a Song to an Existing Playlist

1. Touch and hold on a song.

2. Touch Add to Playlist.

3. Touch the name of the playlist you want to add the song to.

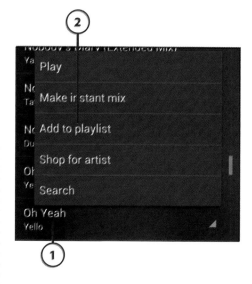

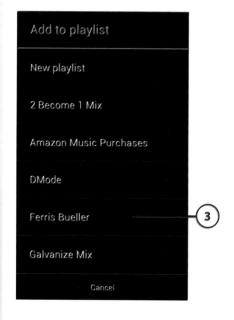

# Rearranging Songs in a Playlist

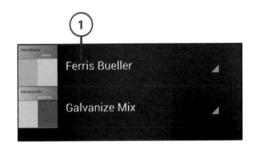

1. Touch a Playlist to show the songs in it.

2. Touch and hold the symbol to the left of a song you want to move. Move that song up and down until it is in the right place, and then release it.

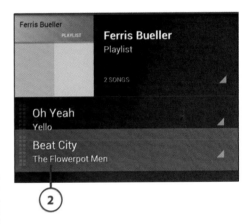

# Delete or Rename a Playlist

1. Touch and hold on the playlist you want to delete or rename.

2. Touch to delete the playlist.

3. Touch to rename the playlist.

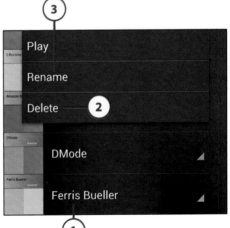

# Listening to Music with No Wireless Coverage

As established earlier in the chapter, if you utilize Google Music to store your music in Google's cloud, when you play that music on your Galaxy Nexus, it is actually streaming over the cellular or Wi-Fi networks. If you know that you are going to be without a signal but still want to listen to your music, follow these steps.

1. Touch the Menu button.

2. Touch Make Available Offline.

3. Touch the check boxes next to songs, artists, playlists, or albums.

4. Touch the check mark to save your selection and start the music download to your Galaxy Nexus.

Indicates how much space is left to store songs for offline listening

# Changing Google Music Settings

1. Touch the Menu button.

2. Touch to show only music you have directly copied to your phone from a computer or chosen to be made available offline.

3. Touch Settings.

4. Touch to change the Google Account being used for Google Music.

5. Touch to show only music stored on your Galaxy Nexus. When this setting is on you see only music you have directly copied to your phone from a computer or chosen to be made available offline.

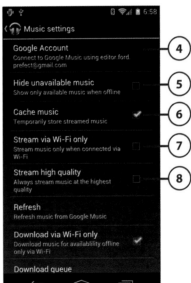

6. Touch to enable or disable caching of streamed music. When this is enabled, music you are listening to is temporarily stored on your Galaxy Nexus. So if you play one of the songs again, it plays it straight from memory.

7. Touch to enable or disable streaming over Wi-Fi only. When this is enabled, you won't be able to play music that is not already stored on your Galaxy Nexus while not connected to a Wi-Fi network.

8. Touch to enable or disable streaming high-quality music. When this option is enabled and you listen to music not already stored on your Galaxy Nexus, the music streams at the highest quality. Be careful when using this option when you're not connected to a Wi-Fi network because highest quality also means more data usage.

9. Touch to manually refresh the list of music shown on your Galaxy Nexus.

10. Touch to enable or disable downloading music over Wi-Fi only. When this option is enabled, if you choose to make music offline that music does not download unless you are connected to a Wi-Fi network.

11. Touch to see the download queue. When you choose to make music available offline, that music is queued for download. You can see the download progress here.

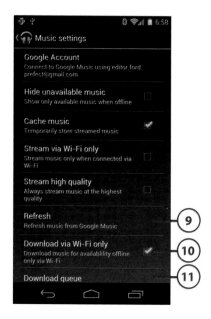

## WHAT'S THE POINT OF DOWNLOADING OR STREAMING OVER WI-FI ONLY?

In some of the settings, you can choose to only download music over Wi-Fi or only stream over Wi-Fi. The reason that these are useful is because Wi-Fi is free. When you download or stream music over the cellular network, it counts against your monthly data plan. If you have a very low monthly data cap, you might want to use one or both of these options to reduce the amount of data that downloading or streaming music uses each month. Probably the best way to save money is to enable streaming over Wi-Fi only (see step 7) and enable downloading music over Wi-Fi only (see step 10). Then while you are at home on Wi-Fi, select the music you want to take offline (see "Listening to Music With No Coverage"). Before you leave home for the day, turn on the setting to only show music you have stored on your phone to (see step 2). Now your music downloads at home, but as you go throughout your day, playing music is free.

## Control Playback from The Lock Screen

You don't have to unlock your Galaxy Nexus to control music while it is playing. Press the Power button and use the onscreen controls to pause or play the song and jump to the previous or next song in the playlist, album, or song list.

**Push the Power button to control your music**

## SYNCHRONIZE MUSIC AND OTHER MEDIA USING A CABLE

If for some reason you don't want to make use of Google Music or you can't because you live in a country where Google Music is not supported, you can synchronize music and other media using a cable (and sometimes over Wi-Fi). A great way to do this is to download an app called doubleTwist. doubleTwist has been providing media synchronization for many smartphones for a while now, and the product is very mature. Head to http://doubleTwist.com to download the Windows or Mac version and head to the Android Market to download the Android app companion.

# Playing and Sharing Videos

The Gallery application enables you to view pictures and video and share pictures and video with people on Facebook, or via MMS, Bluetooth, YouTube, and email. This chapter covers viewing and sharing videos. Read Chapter 9, "Taking, Storing, and Viewing Photos," for information on taking and sharing pictures.

1. Touch the Gallery icon to launch the Gallery application.

2. Touch an album to open it.

3. Touch a video to start playing it. Videos have a little Play icon on them.

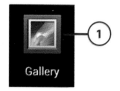

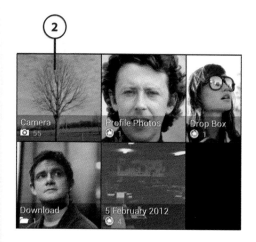

4. Touch the screen while the video is playing to reveal the video controls.

5. Touch to pause or unpause the video.

6. Drag the slider to quickly skip forward and backward.

7. Rotate your Galaxy Nexus sideways to allow the video to fill the screen.

## Sharing Videos

You can share small videos with people from the Gallery application. Here is how.

1. Touch and hold the video you want to share.

2. Touch to share the video on your Facebook wall.

3. Touch to see other ways to share the video.

4. Touch to send the video via Gmail.

5. Touch to send the video via Bluetooth.

6. Touch to send the video as a video text message or MMS.

7. Touch to upload the video to YouTube or send it via email (not Gmail). See the "YouTube" section later in this chapter for more about uploading a video to YouTube.

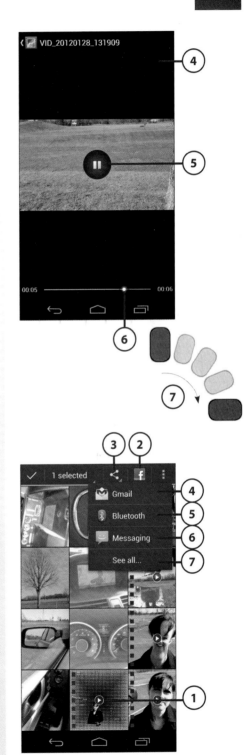

## Small Video Size

You can only share very small videos from your Galaxy Nexus. The video file size normally cannot exceed 3 Mb, which is about one minute of high-quality video, or about two minutes of low-quality video. This is true for all types of video sharing, except MMS; when you share videos via MMS they can only be 30 seconds long. The actual size of the videos that you can send depends on your wireless carrier's limitations.

## Bluetooth Sharing Might Fail

Many phones do not accept incoming Bluetooth files, but devices like computers do. Even on computers, the recipient must configure her Bluetooth configuration to accept incoming files.

## Uploading or Sharing Multiple Videos

You can share or upload multiple videos at the same time, instead of one-by-one. After you touch and hold a video, touch more videos to add them to your list. When you select more than one video to share, however, the option to share on Facebook is disabled because you can only upload videos to Facebook one at a time. After you reduce your list of videos to share back to one, the Facebook sharing option returns.

# Deleting Videos

1. Touch and hold the video you want to delete.

2. Touch the Menu button.

3. Touch Delete.

### Delete Multiple Videos

You can delete multiple videos at the same time. To do this, after you touch and hold to select the first video, touch the other videos you want to delete. You see the number of select items increase in the upper-left corner of the screen. After you have chosen all the videos you want to delete, touch the Menu button and touch Delete.

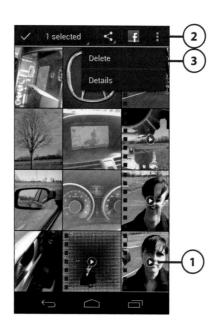

## Gallery App Settings

1. Touch the Menu button.

2. Touch Settings.

3. Touch to edit the settings for your Google account, including turning Photo Sync on or off.

4. Touch to enable or disable synchronizing photos over Wi-Fi only.

---

### What Is Photo Sync?

Photo Sync is a feature that automatically copies all photos you have uploaded from your computer to your Picasa web albums or have uploaded to your Google+ account. If you suddenly upload a lot of photos this way, you might notice a dramatic decrease in battery life as your phone downloads all of the pictures, but under normal use, this should not happen.

## Recording Videos with the Camera Application

The Camera application enables you to take pictures and record video. We cover the video recording feature of the Camera application in this chapter. Using the Camera application to take pictures is covered in Chapter 9.

# Recording Video

1. Touch to launch the Camera app.

2. Touch to choose the camera app mode. The camera app can take still photos, panoramic photos, and record video.

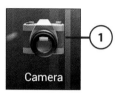

3. Touch the video camera icon to switch to video mode.

4. Rotate your Galaxy Nexus sideways before recording video.

## Why Sideways?

All televisions and computer screens use an aspect ratio of 16:9. This means that they are wider than they are tall. If you don't rotate your phone sideways before recording, when you watch the video on a TV or computer you see a small tall image in the middle of the screen. If you rotate your Galaxy Nexus on its side, the video that you record is also at 16:9 ratio and will fill the TV and computer screen when you watch it.

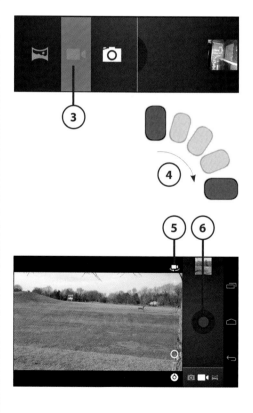

5. Touch to switch between the front-facing and rear-facing cameras.

6. Touch to start recording video.

7. Drag the slider up and down to zoom in and out.

8. Touch to stop recording video.

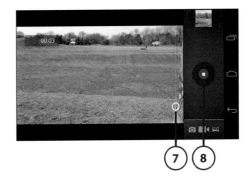

## It's Not All Good

### Zooming Is Fake

Your Galaxy Nexus does not have the ability to zoom. When you move the slider to zoom in, the Camera app is faking the zoom. Although the image appears to be getting larger, what is really going on is the video image is simply being manipulated to appear like it's zooming in. This is commonly called "digital zoom." Optical zoom is when the camera actually zooms using a lens movement, which is something that this camera cannot do.

## Changing Video Settings

Before you record a video, you can change some settings that can alter how the video is recorded.

1. Touch to see the video settings.

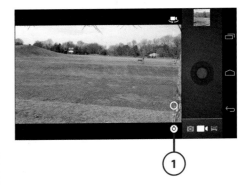

2. Touch to set the flash mode. When you are recording videos, the flash turns into a video camera light so you can turn it on to illuminate a dark scene or turn it off to use natural light.

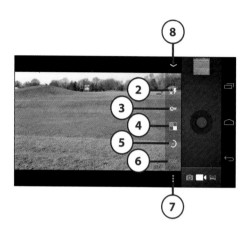

3. Touch to set the White Balance. You can leave it set to Auto or manually set it to some preset levels such as Incandescent, Daylight, Florescent, or Cloudy.

4. Touch to use video effects, which are covered in more detail in the next task.

5. Touch to set a video time-lapse interval. Using time lapse means that the video camera records video at set intervals instead of continuously. You can choose intervals from 1 second to 10 seconds.

6. Touch to set the video quality. The three choices are HD 1080p (the best High Definition video), HD 720p (the lower level of High Definition), or SD 480P (video that is similar to regular non-HD television, or Standard Definition).

7. Touch to enable or disable storing the GPS coordinates of your location when you record the video or to restore your camera settings to the factory defaults.

8. Touch to close the video settings.

# Video Effects

While you are recording video, your Galaxy Nexus can do some cool tricks, such as squeezing the person's face to make their eyes, nose, or mouth either really big or really small. You can also change the video background to make it look like you are in space or in a disco.

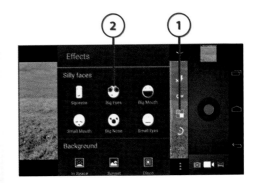

1. Touch the video effects icon.

2. Touch a silly face effect or background. This example uses Big Eyes.

3. As you record the video, your Galaxy Nexus automatically tracks the person and applies the effect, in this case, making the subject's eyes larger.

## It's Not All Good

### Replacing the Backgroung Is Tricky

Your Galaxy Nexus enables you to replace the background of a video with an effect such as "In Space" or "Disco," but to get this right you have to keep the phone completely still. Any slight movement messes up the effect. It works better if you prop your Galaxy Nexus against something so it can't move around and then follow the on-screen instructions to get the background effects right.

# YouTube

Your Galaxy Nexus comes with a YouTube application that enables you to find and watch videos, rate them, add them to your favorites, and share links to YouTube videos. The YouTube application even enables you to upload new videos.

## YouTube Main Screen

1. Touch the YouTube icon to launch the YouTube application.

2. Touch to see the YouTube Home screen.

3. Touch to browse for videos by category.

4. Touch to record a video using your Galaxy Nexus camera and immediately upload it to YouTube.

5. Touch a search for a video on YouTube.

6. Touch to change the YouTube app settings.

7. Touch to see your YouTube account, upload a video already stored in the Gallery app, and see videos you saved as your favorites and the ones you have put in your YouTube Playlists.

8. Touch a video to open it.

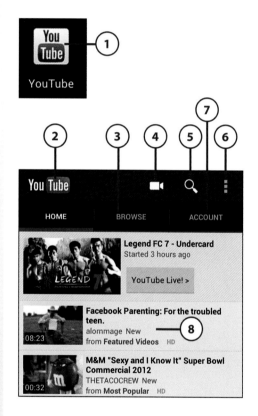

# Browsing for a Video

1. Touch to browse for videos by category.

2. Touch a category.

3. Touch to sort the view by Most Viewed, Top Rated, Most Discussed, and Top Favorited.

4. Touch to show only videos that were uploaded to YouTube today, this week, this month, or choose All Time to show all videos no matter when they were uploaded.

5. Touch a video to open it.

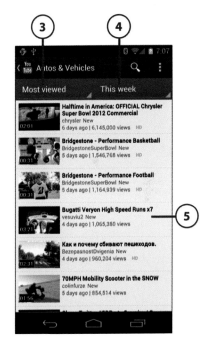

# Playing a Video

While playing a YouTube video, you can rate the video, read video comments, and share the video with someone.

1. Double-tap the video, or rotate your Galaxy Nexus into landscape mode to see the video full screen.

2. Touch to share a link to this video. You can share it on Facebook, Twitter, Google+, or by more traditional ways such as email and text message.

3. Touch to add this video to your favorites, save the video to an existing or new YouTube playlist, or flag the video.

4. Touch to give this video a thumbs up.

5. Touch to give this video a thumbs down.

6. Touch to see videos that are related to this one. YouTube will find videos that are related because of content and keywords.

7. Touch to read comments made about this video and write your own.

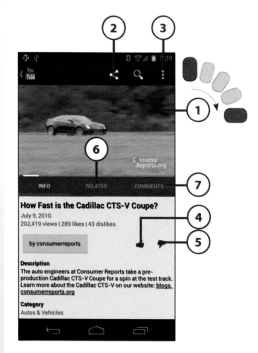

# Record a Video and Upload It

You can record a video with your Galaxy Nexus and immediately upload it to YouTube.

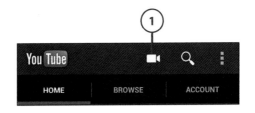

1. Touch to start recording your video.

2. Touch to cancel recording the video if you change your mind.

3. Touch to start and stop recording your video. Refer to the "Recording Videos with the Camera Application" section earlier in this chapter to learn how to change the settings or use effects. When you stop recording you are automatically taken to the next step.

4. Touch your Google account. If you have multiple Google accounts, you might want to use a specific one to upload this video.

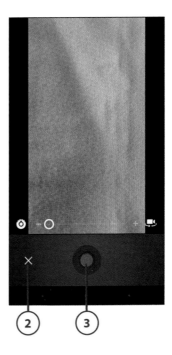

5. Touch to enter a title for your video.

6. Touch to enter a description for your video.

7. Touch to choose whether the video is private, public, or unlisted.

8. Touch to add any tags or keywords so that your video can be found if people search using the tags you enter.

9. Touch to upload your video.

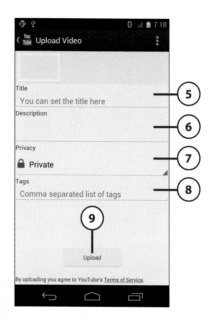

## Upload a Video

You can upload a video to YouTube that you already have saved in the Gallery app. Here is how.

1. Touch the Account tab.

2. Touch the upload icon.

3. Touch a video to select it.

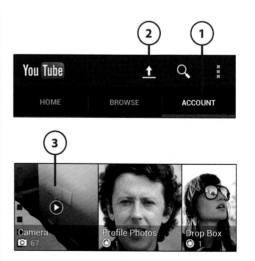

4. Touch to enter a title for your video.

5. Touch to enter a description for your video.

6. Touch to choose whether the video is private, public, or unlisted.

7. Touch to add any tags or key words so that your video can be found if people search using using the tags you enter.

8. Touch to upload your video.

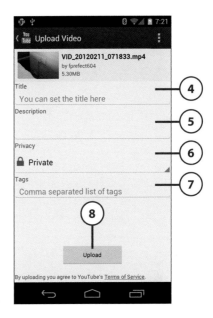

# Changing YouTube Settings

If you want to clear your YouTube search history, or change the Time Filter, you can do this in the YouTube application's settings screen.

1. Touch the Menu button

2. Touch Settings.

3. Touch General Settings.

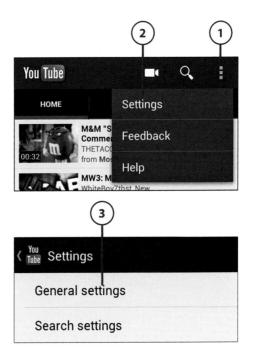

4. Touch to enable or disable high quality on mobile. When enabled, videos start playing in high quality even when you are on a cellular network.

5. Touch to change the video caption font size.

6. Touch to choose when your Galaxy Nexus should upload videos to YouTube. Your choices are Only When on WiFi, and On Any Network.

7. Touch to return to the main settings menu.

8. Touch Search settings.

9. Touch to clear your YouTube search history.

10. Touch to change the SafeSearch filtering options. This allows you to choose whether you want YouTube to filter out certain content. You can select no filtering, moderate filtering, or strict filtering.

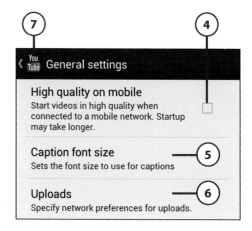

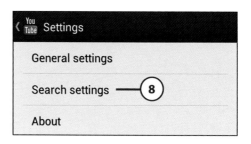

Touch to turn
Wi-Fi on and off

In this chapter, you learn about Galaxy Nexus connectivity capabilities, including Bluetooth, Wi-Fi, VPN, and NFC. Topics include the following:

→ Pairing with Bluetooth devices

→ Connecting to Wi-Fi networks

→ Virtual Private Networks (VPN)

→ Using your Galaxy Nexus as a Wi-Fi Hotspot

→ Using Near Field Communications (NFC)

# Connecting to Bluetooth, Wi-Fi, and VPNs

Your Galaxy Nexus can connect to Bluetooth devices such as headsets, computers, and car in-dash systems, as well as to Wi-Fi networks and 2G and 3G cellular networks. It has all the connectivity you should expect on a great smartphone. Your Galaxy Nexus can also connect to virtual private networks (VPN) for access to secure networks. Your Galaxy Nexus can even share its cellular data connection with other devices over Wi-Fi.

## Connecting to Bluetooth Devices

Bluetooth is a great personal area network (PAN) technology that allows for short distance wireless access to all sorts of devices such as headsets, other phones, computers, and even car in-dash systems for hands-free calling. The following tasks walk you through how to pair your Galaxy Nexus to your device and configure options.

# Pairing with a New Bluetooth Device

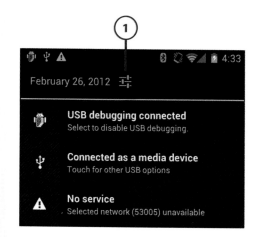

Before you can take advantage of Bluetooth, you need to connect your Galaxy Nexus with that device, which is called pairing. After you pair your Galaxy Nexus with a Bluetooth device, they can connect to each other automatically in the future.

## Put the Bluetooth Device into Pairing Mode First

Before you pair a Bluetooth device to your Galaxy Nexus, you must first put the device into Pairing Mode. If you are pairing with a Bluetooth headset, for example, the process normally involves holding the button on the headset for a certain period of time. Please consult your Bluetooth device's manual on how to put that device into Pairing Mode.

**Your Galaxy Nexus Bluetooth name**

**Discovered Bluetooth devices**

1. Pull down the Notification Bar and touch the Settings icon.

2. Touch Bluetooth under the Wireless & Networks section.

3. Touch Search for Devices if you don't see the device you want to connect to in the list of discovered devices.

4. Touch the Bluetooth device you want to connect to. In this case we are going to connect to the 390Plantronics headset.

5. Touch Device Name to change the name that your Galaxy Nexus uses when it broadcasts on the Bluetooth network.

6. If all went well, your Galaxy Nexus should now be paired with the new Bluetooth device.

—**Successfully paired**

## All Zeros

If you are pairing with an older Bluetooth headset, you might be prompted to enter the passkey. Try using four zeros as the passkey. It normally works. If the zeros don't work, refer to the headset's manual.

## Bluetooth Passkey

If you are pairing with a device that requires a passkey, such as a car in-dash system or a computer, the screen shows a passkey. Make sure the passkey is the same on your Galaxy Nexus and on the device you are pairing with. Touch Pair on your Galaxy Nexus, and confirm the passkey on the device you are pairing with.

—**Touch to confirm the passkey and pair**

## Reverse Pairing

The steps in this section describe how to pair your Galaxy Nexus with a Bluetooth device that is in Pairing Mode, listening for an incoming pairing command. You can pair Bluetooth another way by putting your Galaxy Nexus in Discovery Mode. To do this, touch the Bluetooth name of your Galaxy Nexus on the screen (this is normally "Galaxy Nexus" unless you changed it). Your Galaxy Nexus goes into pairing mode for two minutes.

**— Touch to make your Galaxy Nexus visible for pairing**

# Changing Bluetooth Settings

You can change the name your Galaxy Nexus uses when pairing over Bluetooth, and change the amount of time it remains visible when pairing. Here is how.

1.  Touch the Menu button.

2.  Touch to rename your Galaxy Nexus phone.

3.  Touch to change how long your Galaxy Nexus stays visible when pairing.

4.  Touch to see any files people have sent you over the Bluetooth network.

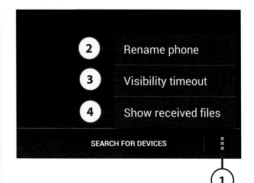

## How Long Should I Stay Visible?

When you choose to change your visibility timeout, you can choose 2 minutes, 5 minutes, 1 hour, or never time out. If you think that the person who wants to pair with you may take more than 2 minutes to do it, then you'll need to change your visibility timeout. Although you can leave the setting on never time out, it is probably not a good idea because every now and then hackers find ways to break into your phone via Bluetooth using a hacker technique called bluesnarfing. This is very rare. More common is a harmless activity called bluejacking where you can send your vCard to someone's phone if they leave their phone visible.

# Changing Bluetooth Device Options

After a Bluetooth device is paired, you can change a few options for some of them. The number of options depends on the Bluetooth device you are connecting to. Some have more features than others.

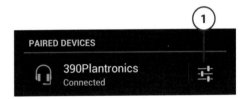

1. Touch the Settings icon to the right of the Bluetooth device.

2. Touch to rename the Bluetooth device to something more friendly.

3. Touch to disconnect and unpair from the Bluetooth device. If you do this, you won't be able to use the device until you redo the pairing as described in the previous task.

4. Touch to enable and disable using this device for phone calls. Sometimes Bluetooth devices have more than one profile. You can use this screen to select which ones you want to use.

## Bluetooth Profiles

Each Bluetooth device can have one or more Bluetooth profiles. Each Bluetooth profile describes certain features of the device. This tells your Galaxy Nexus what it can do when connected to it. A Bluetooth headset normally only has one profile such as Phone Audio. This tells your Galaxy Nexus that it can only use the device for phone call audio. Some devices might have this profile but provide other features such as a Phone Book Access profile that would enable it to synchronize your Galaxy Nexus address book. The latter is typical for car in-dash Bluetooth.

## Quick Disconnect

To quickly disconnect from a Bluetooth device, touch the device on the Bluetooth Settings screen and then touch OK.

# Wi-Fi

Wi-Fi (Wireless Fidelity) networks are wireless networks that run within free radio bands around the world. Your local coffee shop probably has free Wi-Fi, and so do many other places such as airports, train stations, malls, and other public areas. Your Galaxy Nexus can connect to any Wi-Fi network and provide you higher Internet access speeds than the cellular network.

## Connecting to Wi-Fi

The following steps explain how to find and connect to Wi-Fi networks. After you have connected your Galaxy Nexus to a Wi-Fi network, you automatically are connected to it the next time you are in range of that network.

1. Pull down the Notification Bar and touch the Settings icon.

2. Touch WiFi under the Wireless & Networks section.

**3.** Touch to turn Wi-Fi on if the slider is in the off position.

**4.** Touch the name of the Wi-Fi network you want to connect to. If the network does not use any security you can skip to step 7.

**5.** Enter the Wi-Fi network password.

**6.** Touch to connect to the Wi-Fi network.

**7.** If all goes well you see the Wi-Fi network in the list with the word Connected under it.

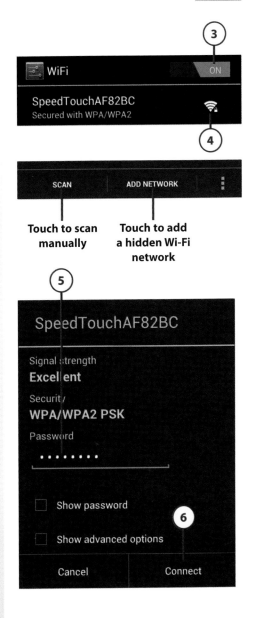

Touch to scan manually

Touch to add a hidden Wi-Fi network

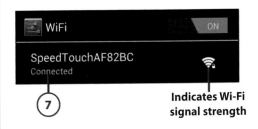

Indicates Wi-Fi signal strength

## Adding a Hidden Network

If the network you want to connect to is not listed on the screen, it might be purposely hidden. If it is hidden, it does not broadcast its name, which is also known as its SSID. You need to touch Add Network, type in the SSID, and choose the type of security that the network uses. You need to get this information from the network administrator ahead of time.

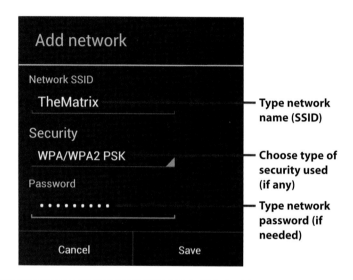

## Can't Connect to Wi-Fi?

If all does not go well, you might be typing the password or encryption key incorrectly. Verify both with the person who owns the Wi-Fi network. Sometimes there is a lot of radio interference that causes problems. If possible, ask the person who owns the Wi-Fi network to change the channel it operates on and try again.

# Wi-Fi Network Options

1. Touch a Wi-Fi network to reveal a pop-up that shows information about your connection to that network.

2. Touch Forget to tell your Galaxy Nexus to not connect to this network in the future.

3. Touch and hold on a Wi-Fi network to reveal two actions.

4. Touch to forget the Wi-Fi network and no longer connect to it.

5. Touch to change the Wi-Fi network password or encryption key that your Galaxy Nexus uses to connect to the network.

# Advanced Wi-Fi Options

You can configure a few advanced Wi-Fi settings that can actually help preserve the battery life of your Galaxy Nexus.

1. Touch the Menu button.

2. Touch Advanced.

3. Touch to enable or disable the ability for your Galaxy Nexus to automatically notify you when it detects a new Wi-Fi network.

4. Touch to change the Wi-Fi sleep policy. This enables you to choose if your Galaxy Nexus should keep its connection to Wi-Fi when the phone goes to sleep.

5. Touch to change which Wi-Fi frequency bands your Galaxy Nexus operates in. You can leave this set to Automatic or manually set it to 2.4 GHZ or 5GHz.

6. Use this Wi-Fi MAC address if you need to provide a network administrator with your MAC address in order to be able to use a Wi-Fi network.

7. This shows the IP address that has been assigned to your Galaxy Nexus when it connected to the Wi-Fi network.

## Should You Keep Wi-Fi on During Sleep?

In step 3 you can choose how your Galaxy Nexus handles its connection to Wi-Fi when it goes to sleep. Because Wi-Fi is much faster and more efficient than 3G, and it is free, you should keep this set to Always. However, battery usage can be affected by always maintaining a Wi-Fi connection, and you might want to set this to Only When Plugged In, which means that if your Galaxy Nexus is not charging, and it goes to sleep, it switches to the cellular network for data. When the phone is charging and it goes to sleep, it stays connected to Wi-Fi. If you set this setting to Never, it means that when your Galaxy Nexus goes to sleep, it switches to using the cellular network for all data. The result is more data being used out of your cellular data bundle, which might cost extra, so be cautious about using this setting.

## WHAT ARE IP AND MAC ADDRESSES?

>>Go Further

A MAC address is a number burned into your Galaxy Nexus that identifies its Wi-Fi adapter. This is called the physical layer because it is a physical adapter. An IP address is a secondary way to identify your Galaxy Nexus. Unlike a MAC address, the IP address can be changed anytime. Modern networks use the IP address when they need to deliver some data to you. Typically when you connect to a network, a device on the network assigns you a new IP address. On home networks, this device is typically your Wi-Fi router.

Some network administrators use a security feature to limit who can connect to their Wi-Fi networks. They set up their networks to only allow connections from Wi-Fi devices with specific MAC addresses. If you are trying to connect to such a network, you have to give the network administrator your MAC address so that he can add it to the allowed list.

# Cellular Networks (GSM Version)

Your Galaxy Nexus can connect to GSM cellular networks in the U.S. and globally.

# Changing Mobile Settings

Your Galaxy Nexus has a few options when it comes to how it connects to cellular (or mobile) networks.

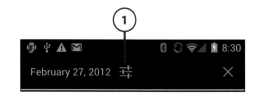

1. Pull down the Notification Bar and touch the Settings icon.

2. Touch More under the Wireless & Networks section.

3. Touch Mobile Networks.

4. Touch to enable or disable cellular data. If this is unchecked, your Galaxy Nexus is only able to use data when connected to a Wi-Fi network.

5. Touch to enable or disable cellular data roaming. If this is unchecked, your Galaxy Nexus does not attempt to use data while you roam away from your home cellular network.

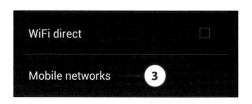

## What Is an APN?

APN stands for Access Point Name. You normally don't have to make changes to APNs, but sometimes you need to enter them manually to access certain features. For example, if you need to use tethering, which is where you connect your laptop to your Galaxy Nexus and your Galaxy Nexus provides Internet connectivity for your laptop, you might be asked by your carrier to use a specific APN. Think of an APN as a gateway to a service.

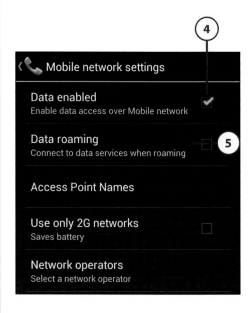

6. Touch to view, edit, and add APNs. It is unlikely that you need to make any APN changes.

7. Touch to enable or disable only using 2G cellular networks. While having this enabled saves battery life, it means you have very, very slow data connectivity.

## Can I Disable Mobile Data?

If you disable mobile data, you can save battery life, however you effectively kill the functionality of any app that needs to be connected all the time, such as instant messaging apps (Yahoo, Google Talk, and so on) or apps like Skype. You also stop receiving email in real time. When this feature is disabled, about five minutes after your Galaxy Nexus goes to sleep, it disconnects from the mobile data network, but it remains connected to the mobile voice network.

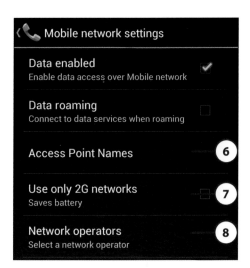

8. Touch to view and choose mobile operators to use.

9. Touch to let your Galaxy Nexus select a network operator to use automatically. If you are roaming outside your home country, the device automatically chooses the carrier. (See the "Why Select Operators Manually?" margin note.)

10. Touch to search for and select mobile operators manually.

11. Touch a mobile operator to register your Galaxy Nexus on that network.

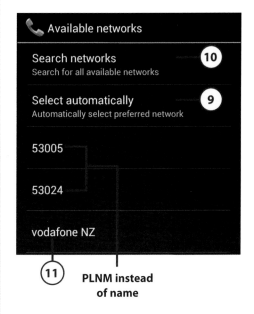

## Why Select Operators Manually?

When you are roaming in your home country, your Galaxy Nexus automatically selects your home cellular provider. When you are roaming outside your home country, your Galaxy Nexus registers on a cellular provider based on its name and how it scores alphabetically. The lowest score will always win. For example a carrier whose name starts with a number is always chosen over carriers whose names start with letters. A carrier whose name starts with the letter *A* is chosen over a carrier whose name starts with the letter *B*, and so on. As you roam, your home carrier might not have a good roaming relationship with a carrier that your Galaxy Nexus has chosen based on its name, so you might want to choose the carrier manually to ensure the best roaming rates and, many times, basic connectivity. You might notice that sometimes carrier names are not displayed. Instead, their operator codes (or PLNMs) are displayed. In the figure, 53024 is actually 2Degrees in New Zealand, and 53005 is Telecom New Zealand.

# Cellular Networks (CDMA Version)

Your Galaxy Nexus can connect to CDMA and LTE cellular networks in the U.S. and in a few other countries that still use CDMA networks. Your Galaxy Nexus has a few options when it comes to how it connects to cellular (or mobile) networks.

1. Pull down the Notification Bar and touch the Settings icon.

2. Touch More under the Wireless & Networks section.

3. Touch Mobile Networks.

4. Touch to enable or disable cellular data. If this is unchecked, your Galaxy Nexus is only able to use data when connected to a Wi-Fi network.

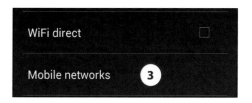

5. Touch to enable or disable cellular data roaming. If this is unchecked, your Galaxy Nexus does not attempt to use data while you roam away from your home cellular network.

6. Touch to enable or disable only using CDMA or 2G cellular networks. Although having this enabled saves battery life, it means you have very, very slow data connectivity.

7. Touch to choose whether to only allow your Galaxy Nexus to use your home CDMA wireless provider, or to choose a CDMA provider automatically when you roam.

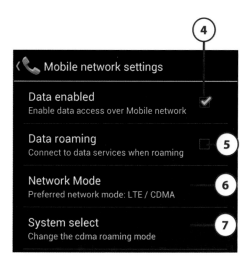

# Virtual Private Networks (VPN)

Your Galaxy Nexus can connect to virtual private networks (VPNs), which are normally used by companies to provide a secure connection to their inside networks or intranets.

# Adding a VPN

Before you add a VPN, you must first
have all the information needed to
set it up on your Galaxy Nexus. Speak
to your network administrator and
get this information ahead of time
to save frustration. This information
includes the type of VPN protocol
used, type of encryption used, and
the name of the host to which you
are connecting.

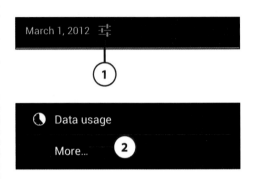

1. Pull down the Notification Bar and
   touch Settings icon.

2. Touch More under the Wireless &
   Networks section.

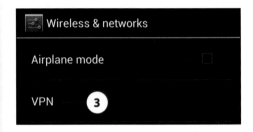

3. Touch VPN.

4. Touch OK to set up a screen lock
   PIN. If you already have a screen
   lock PIN or password, you won't
   be prompted at this point and
   you can proceed to step 8.

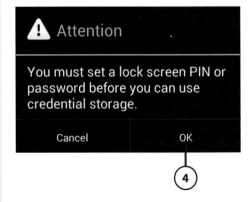

## Why Do You Need to Set a PIN?

If you don't already have a screen
unlock PIN, password, or pattern
set up before you create your first
VPN network connection, you are
prompted to create one. This is
a security measure that ensures
your Galaxy Nexus must first
be unlocked before anyone can
access a stored VPN connection.
Because VPN connections are usu-
ally used to access company data,
this is a good idea.

**5.** Choose either Pattern, PIN, or Password to unlock your Galaxy Nexus. This example uses a simple PIN.

**6.** Enter a screen lock PIN.

**7.** Touch Continue.

**8.** Touch Add VPN Network.

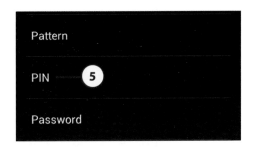

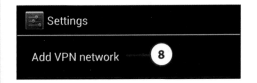

9. Enter a name for your VPN network. You can call it anything like "Work VPN" or the name of the provider like "PublicVPN."

10. Touch to choose the type of security the VPN network uses.

11. Enter the remaining parameters that your network administrator has provided.

12. Touch Save.

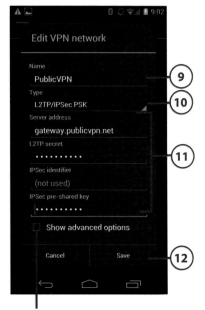

**Touch to set advanced options like DNS and forwarding**

## Connecting to a VPN

After you have created one or more VPN connections, you can connect to them when the need arises.

1. Pull down the Notification bar and touch the Settings icon.

2. Touch More under the Wireless & Networks section.

3. Touch VPN.

4. Touch a pre-configured VPN connection.

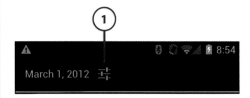

**5.** Follow steps 1–3 in the "Adding a VPN" section to navigate to the VPN Settings. Enter the VPN user-name.

**6.** Enter the VPN password.

**7.** Touch Connect. After you're con-nected to the VPN, you can use your Galaxy Nexus web browser and other applications normally, but you now have access to resources at the other end of the VPN tunnel, such as company web servers or even your company email.

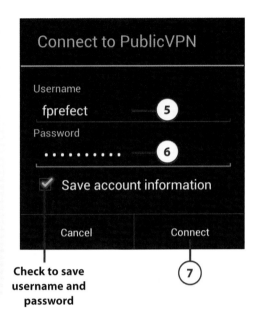

Check to save
username and
password

## How Can You Tell If You Are Connected?

After your Galaxy Nexus successfully connects to a VPN network, you see a key icon in the Notification Bar. This indicates that you are connected. If you pull down the Notification Bar, you can touch the icon to see information about the connection and to disconnect from the VPN.

Connected
to VPN

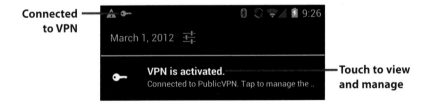

Touch to view
and manage

## Edit or Delete a VPN

You can edit an existing VPN or delete it by touching and holding on the name of the VPN. A window pops up with a list of options.

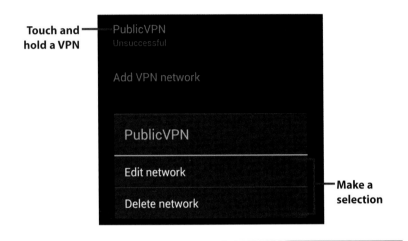

Touch and hold a VPN

Make a selection

# Portable Wi-Fi Hotspot

Your Galaxy Nexus has the ability to share its cellular data connection with up to eight devices over Wi-Fi. Before you use this feature you need to sign up for a tethering plan with your cellular provider, which is normally an extra monthly cost.

## Starting Your Portable Wi-Fi Hotspot

1. Pull down the Notification Bar and touch the Settings icon.

2. Touch More.

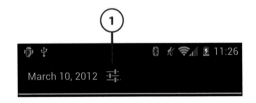

**3.** Touch Tethering & Portable Hotspot.

**4.** Touch Configure WiFi Hotspot.

**5.** Choose a network name (also known as the SSID) for your portable hotspot.

**6.** Touch to choose the type of security to use for your portable hotspot or choose Open to use no security.

**7.** Touch to make the network password visible.

**8.** Enter a password for your portable hotspot if you chose to use a security method in step 6.

**9.** Touch to save your portable hotspot settings.

**10.** Touch to enable your portable hotspot.

**11.** Provide the network name and password (if you chose to use security) to anyone you want to make use of your portable hotspot to connect to the Internet.

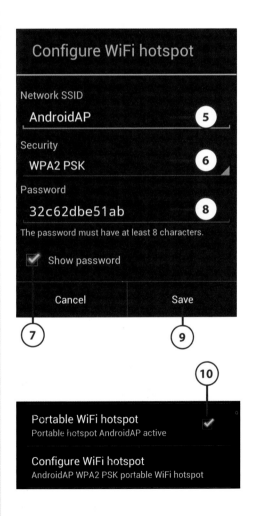

## It's Not All Good

**No Control over Portable Hotspot**

After you start your portable hotspot, you have absolutely no control over it. One would expect to have the ability to change the number of people who could connect, and maybe see the list of devices that are connected, but you aren't able to do that.

### Turn Your Portable Hotspot Off

To turn your hotspot off, simply uncheck the checkbox.

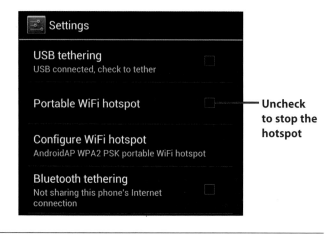

**Uncheck to stop the hotspot**

# Bluetooth Tethering

Your Galaxy Nexus has the ability to share its cellular data connection with a computer via Bluetooth. Before you use this feature,w you must first pair the computer to your Galaxy Nexus via Bluetooth. Refer to the "Connecting to Bluetooth Devices" section earlier in this chapter.

1. Pull down the Notification Bar and touch the Settings icon.

2. Touch More.

3. Touch Tethering & Portable Hotspot.

4. Touch to turn on Bluetooth tethering. Touch again to turn it off.

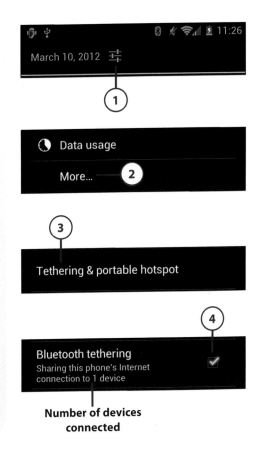

# Near Field Communications (NFC)

Your Galaxy Nexus has the ability to swap data via its Near Field Communications (NFC) radio with other phones that use NFC or read data that is stored on NFC tags. You can also use NFC to pay for items you have purchased. Here is how to start using NFC.

## >>>Go Further

# WHAT IS NFC?

NCF stands for Near Field Communications and is a standard that enables devices such as mobile phones to swap information or simply read information. Think of NFC as a much lower-power version of RFID (Radio Frequency Identification), which has been used for decades in applications like electronic tolls, or etoll payments (when you drive through toll plazas and have the money automatically deducted from your account). The only difference is with NFC, you must bring the two devices within about an inch from each other before they can communicate.

Your Galaxy Nexus has an NFC radio in it, but strangely it cannot yet work with Google's Wallet application that allows you to pay for purchases by holding your phone near a reader at the check-out isle. Let's hope that they allow this in the near future because this is the exact kind of use that will make NFC a well-adopted and popular technology. You can use NFC to read NFC tags, swap information between two NFC-enabled devices (such as two NFC-enabled phones), and send information to another phone or device. As more phones start shipping with NFC built-in, the more this technology will become useful.

# Enabling NFC

1. Pull down the Notification Bar and touch the Settings icon.

2. Touch More.

3. Touch to enable NFC data exchange.

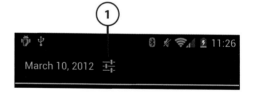

# Using NFC

1. Put the back of your Galaxy Nexus about one inch from the back of another NFC enabled phone, an NFC tag, or reader.

2. The screen dims to indicate that your Galaxy Nexus is reading data from the other NFC device.

3. If the data your Galaxy Nexus reads is a web page link, it automatically opens the web browser and loads that page.

4. If the data your Galaxy Nexus reads is a contact card, it prompts you to choose which account the contact card must be created in.

Create contact under account

editor.ford.prefect@gmail.com
Google

fprefect@humanoidsoftware.
onmicrosoft.com
Corporate

**Choose account**

Touch to open
Gmail email only

Touch to open
email

In this chapter, you learn about your Galaxy Nexus email applications for Gmail and other email accounts such as POP3, IMAP, and even Microsoft Exchange. Topics include the following:

→ Sending and receiving email
→ Working with attachments
→ Working with Gmail labels
→ Changing settings

# Emailing

Your Galaxy Nexus has two email programs: the Gmail app, which only works with Gmail, and the Email app that works with POP3, IMAP, and Microsoft Exchange accounts.

## Gmail

When you first set up your Galaxy Nexus, you set up a Gmail account. The Gmail application enables you to have multiple Gmail accounts, which is useful if you have a business account and a personal account.

# Adding a Google Account

When you first set up your Galaxy Nexus, you added your first Google (Gmail) account. The following steps describe how to add a second account.

1. Touch to open the Gmail app.

2. Touch the Menu button.

3. Touch Settings.

4. Touch Add Account.

5. Touch Sign In.

6. Enter your existing Google account name. This is your Gmail address.

7. Enter your existing Google password.

8. Touch Sign In

## What If I Don't Have a Second Google Account?

If you don't already have a second Google account but want to set one up, in step 5, touch Get a Google Account. Your Galaxy Nexus will walk you through the steps of setting up a new Google account.

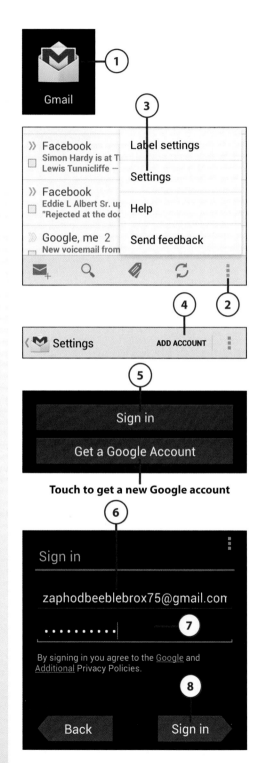

Gmail

»  Facebook
Simon Hardy is at Tl
Lewis Tunnicliffe —

»  Facebook
Eddie L Albert Sr. up
"Rejected at the doc

»  Google, me  2
New voicemail from

Label settings

Settings

Help

Send feedback

Settings        ADD ACCOUNT

Sign in

Get a Google Account

**Touch to get a new Google account**

Sign in

zaphodbeeblebrox75@gmail.com

· · · · · · · · · ·

By signing in you agree to the Google and Additional Privacy Policies.

Back            Sign in

## What's Google+?

When you get to step 9 you see a button to join Google+. This is inviting you to join Google+ using the Google account you are logging in with. You might already use Google+ on another Google account and might not want to use it with this account. In that case, simply touch Not Now. Google+ is a social network just like Facebook and MySpace, and you might want to join as it is growing and becoming more popular.

9. Touch Not Now.

10. Select what components of your Google account you want to synchronize with your Galaxy Nexus.

11. Touch Next to finish the Google account setup.

## Why Multiple Google Accounts?

You are probably wondering why you would want multiple Google accounts. Isn't one good enough? Actually it is not that uncommon to have multiple Google accounts. It can be a way to compartmentalize your life between work and play. You might run a small business using the one account, but email only friends with another. Your Galaxy Nexus supports multiple accounts but still enables you to interact with them in one place.

**Touch to join Google+**

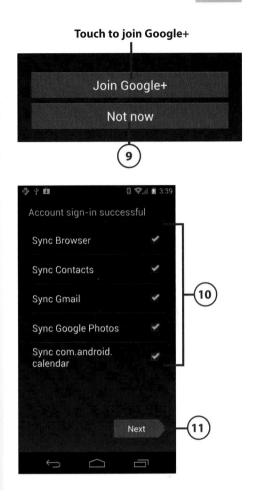

# Navigating the Gmail App

Let's take a quick look at the Gmail app and learn how to navigate the main screen.

1. Touch the Gmail icon to launch the app.

2. Touch to switch between Gmail accounts (if you use more than one) or switch from the Inbox label to one of your other labels. (See the "Stars and Labels" note for more information.)

3. Indicates how many unread messages you have in the selected label.

4. Touch the Menu button to see the menu.

5. Touch to manage your labels including changing which labels synchronize to your Galaxy Nexus.

6. Touch to compose a new email.

7. Touch to search the current label for an email.

8. Touch to manually refresh the current view.

9. Touch to manage your labels.

10. Touch the star to add the email to the Starred label.

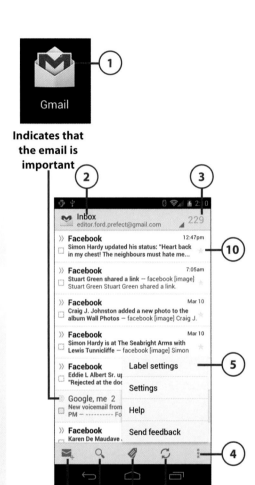

Indicates that the email is important

## Stars and Labels

Gmail allows you to use stars and labels to help organize your email. In most email clients you can create folders in your mailbox to help you organize your emails. For example you might create a folder called "emails from the boss" and move any emails you receive from your boss to that folder. Gmail doesn't use the term folders; it uses the term labels instead. You can create labels in Gmail and choose an email to label. When you do this, it actually moves it to a folder with that label, but to you, the email has a label distinguishing it from other emails. Any email that you mark with a star is actually just getting a label called "starred." But when viewing your Gmail, you see the yellow star next to an email. People normally add a star to an email as a reminder of something important.

## Composing Gmail Email

1. Touch the Compose icon.

2. Touch to change the Gmail account from which the message is being sent (if you have multiple Gmail accounts).

3. Type names in the To field. If the name matches someone in your Contacts, a list of choices is displayed and you can touch a name to select it.

## Can You Carbon Copy (Cc) and Blind Carbon Copy(Bcc)?

While you are composing your email you can add recipients to the To field as described in step 3, but there are no Carbon Copy (Cc) and Blind Carbon Copy (Bcc) fields shown. However, you can add these fields by touching the Menu button and touching Add Cc/Bcc. After you do that, the Cc and Bcc fields are displayed.

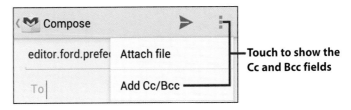

4. Type a subject for your email.

5. Type the body of the email.

6. Touch to send the email.

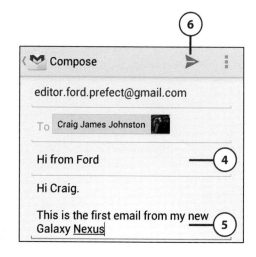

## Add Picture Attachments

Before sending an email, you can add one or more picture attachments. The Gmail app does not allow you to attach other kinds of attachments—just pictures that are in the Gallery app. Here is how to add picture attachments.

1. Touch the Menu button.

2. Touch Attach File.

3. Navigate the Gallery App to find the picture you want to attach.

4. Attachments are listed just below the subject line.

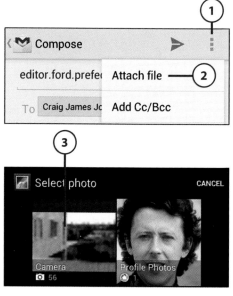

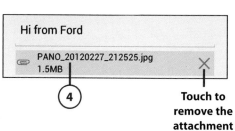

**Touch to remove the attachment**

# Reading Gmail Email

1. Touch an email to open it.

2. Touch to expand the original email if the email you are reading is a reply.

3. Touch to reply to the sender of the email. This does not reply to anyone in the Cc field.

4. Touch the Menu button to do a Reply All (reply to all recipients) or Forward the email.

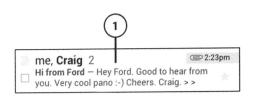

## What Are Conversations?

Conversations are Gmail's version of email threads. When you look at the main view of the Gmail app, you are seeing a list of email conversations. The conversation might have only one email in it, but to Gmail that's a conversation. As you and others reply to that original email, Gmail groups those emails in a thread, or conversation.

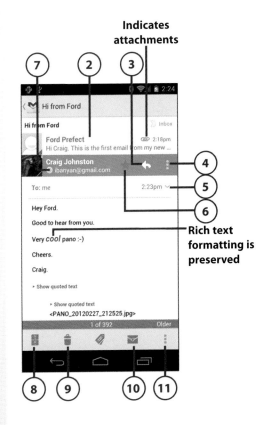

Indicates attachments

Rich text formatting is preserved

5. Touch to expand the email header to see all recipients and all other email header information.

6. Touch to "star" the message, or move it to the "starred" label.

7. Indicates whether the sender of the email is online using Google Talk (GTalk) if that person is in your GTalk buddy list.

8. Touch to move the email to the Gmail Archive folder.

9. Touch to permanently delete the email.

10. Touch to mark the email as unread and return to the email list view.

11. Touch the Menu button to take more actions on the message.

12. Touch to report the email as spam.

13. Touch to mute the email conversation. Once muted, you will no longer see emails in the conversation.

14. Touch to mark the message as not important or important.

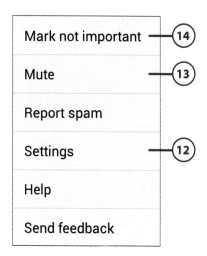

## What Is Important?

Gmail tries to automatically figure out which of the emails you receive are important. As it learns it might get it wrong. If an email is marked as important but it is not important, you can change the status to not important manually as described in step 14. Important emails have a yellow arrow whereas emails that are not important have a clear arrow.

## What Happens to Your Spam?

When you mark an email in Gmail as Spam, two things happen. Firstly it gets a label called Spam. Secondly a copy of that email is sent to Gmail's Spam servers so they are now aware of a possible new spam email that is circulating around the Internet. Based on what the servers see for all Gmail users, they block that spam email from reaching other Gmail users. So the bottom line is that you should always mark spam emails as Spam because it helps all of us.

# Gmail Settings

You can customize the way Gmail accounts work on your Galaxy Nexus including changing the email signature and choosing which labels synchronize.

1. Touch the Menu button.

2. Touch Settings.

---

## Email Signature

An email signature is a bit of text that is automatically added to the bottom of any emails you send from your Galaxy Nexus. It is added when you compose a new email, reply to an email, or forward an email. A typical use for a signature is to automatically add your name and maybe some contact information at the end of your emails. Email signatures are sometimes referred to as email footers.

---

3. Touch General Preferences.

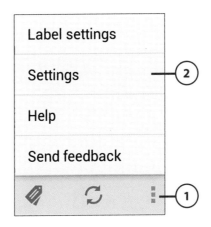

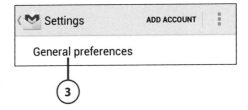

4. Touch to enable or disable confirmation before deleting a message or entire conversation.

5. Touch to enable or disable confirmation before archiving a message or entire conversation.

6. Touch to enable or disable confirmation before sending an email.

7. Touch to enable or disable making Reply All the default action when replying to emails. Normally only Reply is used. Reply All replies to the sender and all recipients.

8. Touch Auto-advance to select which screen your Galaxy Nexus must show after you delete or archive and email. Your choices are Newer Conversation, Older Conversation, and Conversation List.

9. Touch to select the size of the text used when reading emails. Your choices range from Tiny to Huge.

10. Touch to enable or disable hiding the checkboxes in the Conversation List. When this is not enabled, there are always checkboxes next to emails in the conversation list. This enables you to select more than one email and take action on it. If you enable this, the checkboxes are hidden, forcing you to touch and hold to select multiple messages.

11. Scroll down for more options.

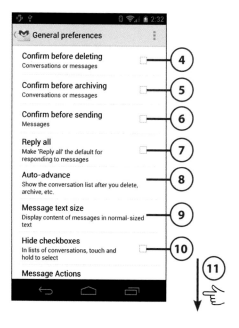

**12.** Touch to change the behavior of the blue message actions bar as you scroll through a message. Your choices are to keep it at the top of the screen as you scroll, only keep it at the top of the screen when in portrait mode, or let it scroll up with the message as you scroll.

**13.** Touch to clear the Gmail search history.

**14.** Touch to restore the setting for whether to automatically load pictures when reading email. By default this is set to off.

**15.** Touch to return to the main Settings screen.

**16.** Touch one of your Gmail accounts to change settings specific to that account.

## What Is the Priority Inbox?

Google recently introduced the Priority Inbox as a way to automatically figure out which emails are important to you and place them in a folder called Priority Inbox. It does this by analyzing which emails you open and reply to. If it makes a mistake, you can mark a message as less important or more important. Over time, Google's handle on which emails are important to you gets more accurate. Because the Priority Inbox probably has the most important emails, you might want to open it first and then go to the regular Inbox later to handle less important emails. Read more about the Priority Inbox at http://mail.google.com/mail/help/priority-inbox.html.

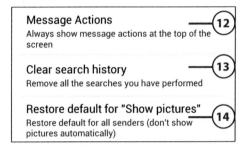

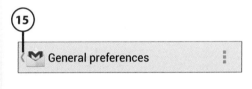

**17.** Touch to enable or disable showing your Priority Inbox instead of your regular Inbox when opening the Gmail app.

**18.** Touch to enable or disable notifications when new email arrives for this Gmail account.

**19.** Touch to select how to get notified when new email arrives for this account.

**20.** Touch to enter a signature that will appear at the end of all emails composed using this account.

**21.** Touch to change how this account is synchronized, what is synchronized, or remove it entirely.

**22.** Touch to select how many days of mail to synchronize with your Galaxy Nexus.

**23.** Touch to manage Labels. See more about managing labels in the next section.

**24.** Scroll down for more options.

**25.** Touch to enable or disable downloading attachments while connected to a Wi-Fi network.

**26.** Touch to return to the main Settings screen.

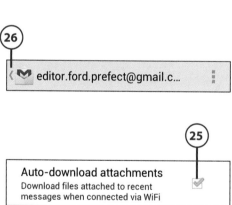

# Managing Gmail Labels

Gmail Labels are Google's name for email folders. You can manage how each of them synchronize and alert you. Here is how.

1. Touch the Inbox label.

2. Touch Show All Labels.

3. Touch Manage Labels.

4. Touch a label to manage it.

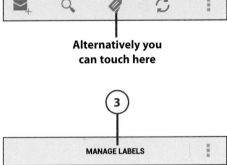

**Alternatively you can touch here**

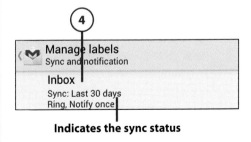

**Indicates the sync status**

5. Touch to enable synchronization of this label to your Galaxy Nexus and designate whether to synchronize 30 days of email or all email. When synchronization is enabled, the rest of the settings on this screen become available.

6. Touch to enable or disable being notified when new email arrives in this label.

7. Touch to select the ringtone that plays when you are notified of new email in this label.

8. Touch to choose whether to also vibrate when new email arrives in this label.

9. Touch to enable or disable notifying you once when multiple emails arrive in this label, as opposed to notifying for each one.

10. Touch to return to the list of labels.

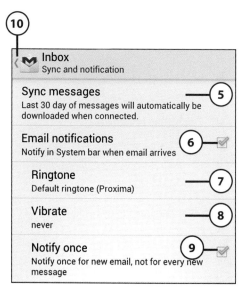

# Email Application

The Email application supports all email accounts with the exception of Gmail. This includes any corporate email accounts that use Microsoft Exchange or corporate emails systems such as Lotus Domino/Notes that have an ActiveSync gateway. In addition to corporate email accounts, the Email application also supports POP3 and IMAP accounts. These are typically hosted by your Internet service provider (ISP), but also by companies such as Yahoo! or Hotmail.

## Adding a Corporate Email Account

Chapter 1, "People (Contacts)," covers adding a corporate email account in the "Adding Accounts" section. Please flip back to Chapter 1 if you want to add a corporate account.

# Adding a New POP3 or IMAP Account

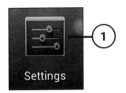

1. Touch the Settings icon.

2. Touch Accounts & Sync.

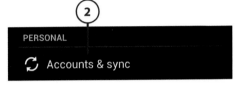

3. Touch Add Account.

4. Touch Email.

5. Enter your email address.

6. Enter your password.

7. Touch Next.

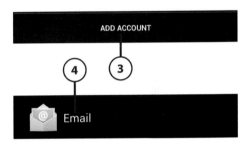

## Why Manual Setup?

Your Galaxy Nexus tries to figure out the settings to set up your email account. This works most of the time when you are using common email providers such as Yahoo! or Hotmail. It also works with large ISPs such as Comcast, Road Runner, Optimum Online, and so on. It might not work for smaller ISPs, or in smaller countries, or if you have created your own website and set up your own email. In these cases, you need to set up your email manually.

8. Touch POP3 or IMAP. IMAP has more intelligence to it, so select that option where possible.

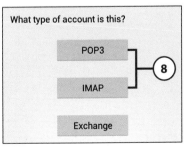

9. Ensure that the information on this screen is accurate.

10. Touch Next.

## Where Can I Find This Information?

If you need to manually set up your email account, you must have a few pieces of information. Always check your ISP's or email service provider's website and look for instructions on how to set up your email on a computer or smartphone. This is normally under the support section of the website.

## Username and Password

On the Incoming Server and Outgoing Server screens, your username and password should already be filled out because you typed them in earlier. If not, enter them.

11. Ensure that the information on this screen is accurate.

12. Touch Next.

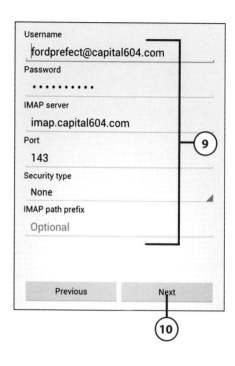

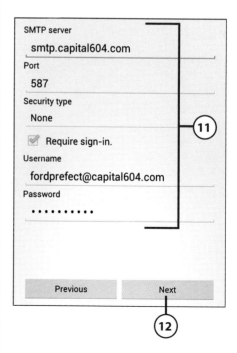

13. Touch to change the frequency in which email from this account synchronizes to your Galaxy Nexus.

14. Touch to check the box if you want email to be sent from this account by default.

15. Touch to check the box if you want to be notified when new email arrives into this account.

16. Touch to check the box if you want email to synchronize between this account and your Galaxy Nexus.

17. Touch to check the box if you want email to be automatically downloaded when you are connected to a Wi-Fi network.

18. Touch Next.

19. Enter a friendly name for this account, such as "Work Email."

20. Enter your full name or the name you want to be displayed when people receive emails sent from this account.

21. Touch Next to save the settings for this account and return to the Add Accounts screen.

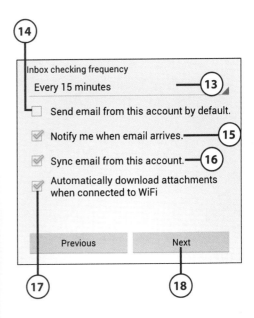

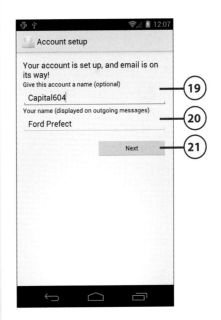

## Be Secure If You Can

If your mail provider supports email security such as SSL or TLS, you should strongly consider using it. If you don't, emails you send and receive go over the Internet in plain readable text. Using SSL or TLS encrypts the emails as they travel across the Internet so nobody can read them. Set this under the Advanced settings for the Incoming and Outgoing Servers.

# Working with the Email App

Now that you have added two new accounts, you can start using the Email application. Everything you do in the Email application is the same for every email account. The Email app enables you to either work with email accounts separately or in a combined view.

## Navigating the Email Application

Before you learn how to compose or read emails, you should become familiar with the Email application.

1. Touch to launch the Email app.

2. Touch to switch between email accounts or select the Combined view, which shows all emails from all accounts.

3. Indicates the number of unread emails in the current folder.

4. Touch the star to mark an email as a flagged.

5. Each color represents a specific email account.

6. Check boxes next to emails to select more than one. Then you can take actions against multiple emails at once, such as Mark as Read, Flag, Delete, or Move to a new folder.

7. Touch the Menu button to change the Email app settings.

8. Touch to switch to a different folder in the mailbox you are viewing.

9. Touch to compose a new email.

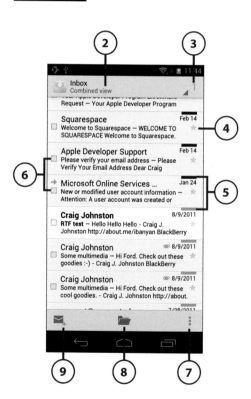

## Composing Email

1.  Touch to compose a new email.

2.  Enter one or more recipients. As you type, your Galaxy Nexus tries to guess who you want to address the message to. If you see the correct name, touch it to select it. This includes names stored on your Galaxy Nexus and in your company's corporate address book

**Indicates the mail account being used**

### It's Not All Good

**Cannot Change Account Being Used**

While composing an email you cannot change the account that is being used to send the email. It is visually indicated on the screen but you cannot modify it. The default account is always used. See the "Email Settings" section later in the chapter to find out how to change the default account.

3.  Enter a subject.

4.  Enter the body of the message.

5.  Touch to send the message.

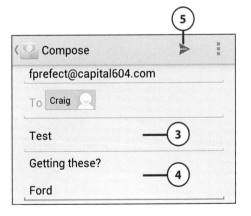

## Can You Carbon Copy (Cc) and Blind Carbon Copy (Bcc)?

While you are composing your email, you can add recipients to the To field as shown in step 3; however, there are no Carbon Copy (Cc) and Blind Carbon Copy (Bcc) fields shown. You can add these fields by touching the Menu button and touching Add Cc/Bcc. After you do that, the Cc and Bcc fields are displayed.

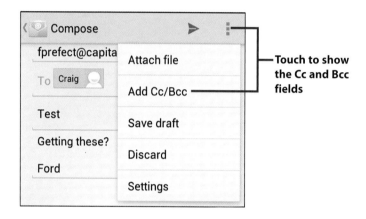

**Touch to show the Cc and Bcc fields**

## Add Attachments

Before you send your message, you might want to add one or more attachments. Unfortunately, you can only attach pictures from the Gallery.

1. Touch the Menu button.

2. Touch Attach File.

3. Select a picture to attach.

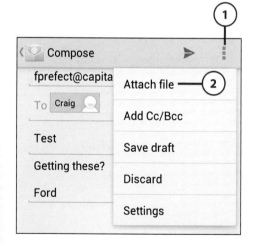

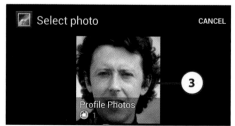

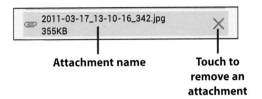

**Attachment name**    **Touch to remove an attachment**

## Can You Attach Other Files?

Although the Gmail app and the Email app actually support any attachment type, the apps themselves only let you attach pictures. To send other attachment types via Gmail or Email, you must install a file manager app such as ASTRO. Browse your Galaxy Nexus to find the file, touch and hold the file, and choose Send. The send method options display. Choose Gmail or Email and a new email is created with the file attached.

# Reading Email

Reading messages in the Email application is the same regardless of which account the email has come to.

1.  You receive a notification in the status bar letting you know that there is a new email.

2.  Touch to reply to the sender of the email. This does not reply to anyone in the Cc field.

3.  Touch the Menu button to do a Reply All (reply to all recipients) or Forward the email.

4.  Touch to expand the email header to see all recipients and all other email header information.

5.  Touch to mark the message as "starred" or "flagged" (for corporate email).

6.  Indicates whether the sender of the email is online using Google Talk (GTalk) if that person is in your GTalk buddy list.

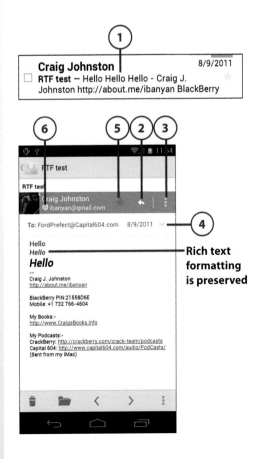

**Rich text formatting is preserved**

**7.** Touch to move the email to a folder.

**8.** Touch to delete the message.

**9.** Touch the Menu button to mark the message as unread or change settings for the Email app. See the next section for more on the Email app settings.

**10.** Touch to go to the previous email.

**11.** Touch to go to the next email.

# Email App Settings

**1.** Touch the Menu button.

**2.** Touch Settings.

**3.** Touch General.

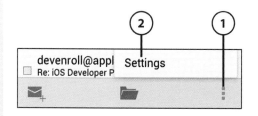

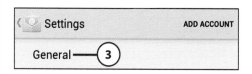

4. Touch to change how Auto-advance works. You can choose to either advance to a newer message, older message, or back to the message list.

5. Touch to change the size of the font used when reading messages. Your choices range from Tiny to Huge.

6. Touch to check the box if you want the default action to be Reply-All instead of Reply when reading a message.

7. Touch to restore the default for "Show pictures." By default pictures do not load when you open messages, but you might have changed this for a message you received. This sets it back to the default setting of not showing pictures.

8. Touch to go back to the main Settings screen.

8     4

Settings            ADD ACCOUNT

**APPLICATION**

Auto-advance
Choose which screen to show after you delete a message

Message text size     5
Normal-sized text

Reply all
Make 'Reply all' the default for responding to messages

Restore default for "Show pictures"
Restore default for all senders (don't show pictures automatically)

7     6

## POP/IMAP Account Settings

1. Touch a POP or IMAP account.

1

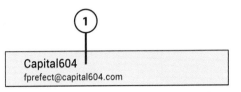

Capital604
fprefect@capital604.com

2. Touch to change the account name.

3. Touch to change the name that recipients see when you send them email from this account.

4. Touch to add an email signature or edit the one you already have.

5. Touch to add or edit Quick Responses.

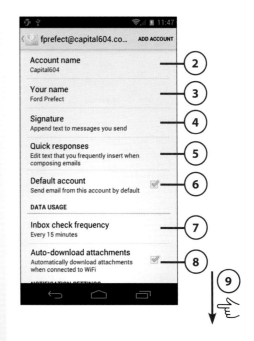

## Quick Responses

Quick Responses are words, phrases, sentences, or paragraphs of text that you create ahead of time and save as Quick Reponses. While you are composing an email you can choose to insert one or more of your Quick Responses. The idea is that it saves on typing the same things over and over.

6. Touch to check the box if you want this account to be used as the default account when composing email.

7. Touch to change the frequency at which the Email app checks this account's Inbox for new email.

8. Touch to check the box if you want attachments to automatically download while you are connected to a Wi-Fi network.

9. Scroll down for more settings.

10. Touch to check the box if you want notifications when new email arrives in this account's Inbox.

11. Touch to choose the ringtone that plays when your are notified of new email for this account.

12. Touch to choose whether your Galaxy Nexus also vibrates when the notification ringtone plays.

13. Touch to change the incoming mail server settings for this account. This includes your account username and password if this has changed.

14. Touch to change the outgoing mail server settings for this account. This includes your account username and password if this has changed.

15. Touch to remove this account.

16. Touch to return to the Settings main screen.

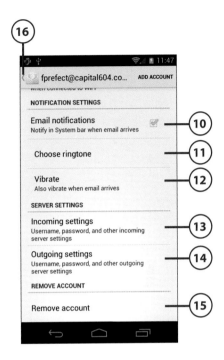

## Corporate Account Settings

You are able to change your email signature. You can also control what components to synchronize and how often they synchronize.

1. Touch a corporate account.

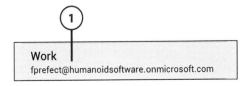

2. Touch to change the account name.

3. Touch to change the name that recipients see when you send them email from this account.

4. Touch to change an email signature or edit the one you already have.

5. Touch to add or edit Quick Responses.

6. Touch to check the box if you want this account to be used as the default account when composing email.

7. Touch to change the frequency at which the Email app checks this account's Inbox for new email. You can also choose Push, which means that emails are pushed to your Galaxy Nexus in real time as they arrive in your corporate Inbox.

8. Touch to choose how many days of email to synchronize to your Galaxy Nexus. You can choose between One Day and One Month, or choose All to synchronize every email ever received.

9. Scroll down for more settings.

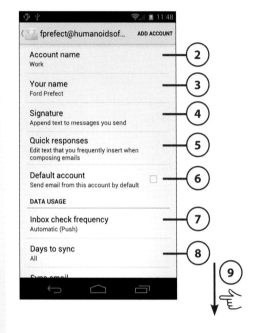

10. Touch to check the box if you want email to synchronize to your Galaxy Nexus from this corporate account.

11. Touch to check the box if you want contacts to synchronize to your Galaxy Nexus from this corporate account.

12. Touch to check the box if you want the calendar to synchronize to your Galaxy Nexus from this corporate account.

13. Touch to check the box if you want attachments to automatically download while you are connected to a Wi-Fi network.

14. Touch to check the box if you want notifications when new email arrives in this account's Inbox.

15. Touch to choose the ringtone that plays when your are notified of new email for this account.

16. Touch to choose whether your Galaxy Nexus also vibrates when the notification ringtone plays.

17. Scroll down for more settings.

18. Touch to change the incoming mail server settings for this account. This includes your account username and password if this has changed.

19. Touch to remove this account.

20. Touch to return to the Settings main screen.

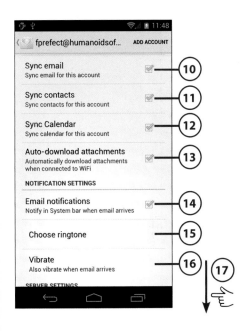

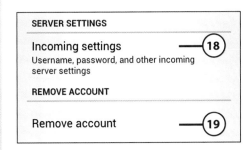

Multiple browser
tabs

In this chapter, you learn about browsing the World Wide Web and using the browser capabilities of your Galaxy Nexus. Topics include the following:

→ Bookmarking websites

→ Sharing websites with your friends

→ Keeping track of sites you have visited

→ Using GPS and browsing together

# Browsing the Web

Your Galaxy Nexus has a fully featured web browser for a smartphone. In fact, the experience using the Galaxy Nexus browser is similar to using a desktop browser, just with a smaller screen. You can bookmark sites, hold your Galaxy Nexus sideways to fit more onto the screen, and even share your GPS location with sites.

## Navigating with Browser

Let's dive right in and cover how to run Browser and use all of its features. Your Galaxy Nexus browser can be customized, share your GPS location, enable you to bookmark sites, and keep your browsing history.

1. Touch the Browser icon on the Home screen.

2. Touch to type in a new web address. Some websites move the web page up to hide the address field. When this happens, you can drag the web page down to reveal the address bar again.

3. Touch to manage Browser's bookmarks, history, and saved pages and to work with browser tabs. (See the next sections for information on bookmarks, history, and tabs.)

4. Touch to go back to the previous page on a website.

5. Touch the Menu button see more options for working with a web page.

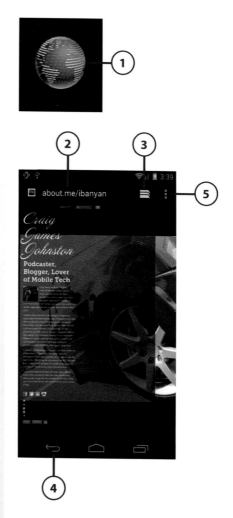

# Web Page Options

While a web page is open, you have a
number of options such as saving the
page to bookmarks and finding text
on a web page.

1. Touch the Menu button.

2. Touch to manually refresh the
   web page.

3. Touch to save the current page to
   your bookmarks.

4. Touch to share the link to the
   current page using a number of
   options including email, Twitter,
   and Facebook.

5. Touch to search the current web
   page for specific text.

6. Touch to force the current website
   to show the desktop web view
   instead of a mobile view.

7. Touch to save the current web
   page so that you can read it even
   with no network connection.

8. Touch to change the web browser
   settings.

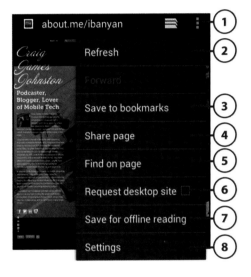

# Browser Tricks

Your Galaxy Nexus has some unique tricks to help you browse regular websites on a small screen.

**Portrait**

**Landscape**

1. Rotate your Galaxy Nexus on its side, which puts the tablet into what's called *landscape orientation*. Your Galaxy Nexus automatically switches the screen to landscape mode.

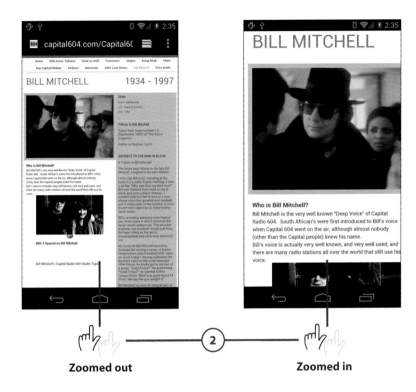

**Zoomed out**                                    **Zoomed in**

2.  Double-tap the screen to zoom in and out.

## Pinch to zoom

An alternative way to zoom, which allows you to actually zoom in much further is to place your thumb and forefinger on the screen and spread them apart to zoom in, and move them back together to zoom out.

# Managing Bookmarks, Saved Pages, and History

Your Galaxy Nexus enables you to bookmark your favorite websites. It also keeps track of where you have browsed and can show you your browsing history broken up by days, weeks, and months, and allows you to read web pages offline.

1. Touch the tabs icon.
2. Touch the star icon.

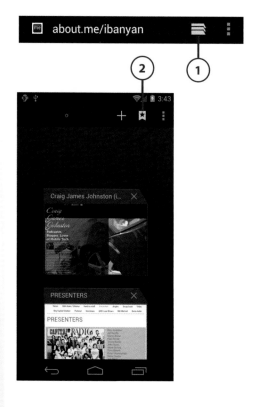

## Bookmarks

1. Touch Bookmarks.

2. Indicates bookmarks that are saved locally on your Galaxy Nexus.

3. Touch a bookmark to load that website.

4. Touch and hold a bookmark to perform extra functions including editing it.

The account to which the bookmarks are synchronized

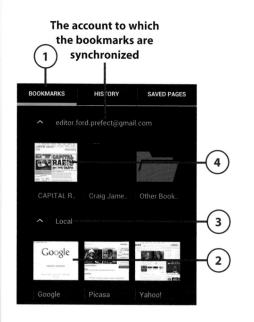

5. Touch to open the bookmark in the current browser tab.

6. Touch to open the bookmark in a new browser tab.

7. Touch to edit the bookmark.

8. Touch to add the bookmark to the Home screen of your Galaxy Nexus.

9. Touch to share the link using varies methods including email, Twitter, and Facebook.

10. Touch to copy the link to the clipboard. After it is in the clipboard, you can paste it into any other screen, such as the body of an email message.

11. Touch to delete the bookmark.

12. Touch to set the bookmark as the home page of the web browser. The home page is always loaded when you start the web browser.

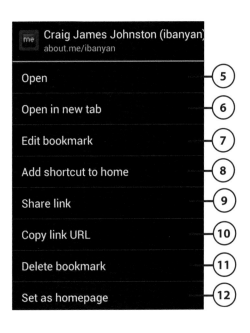

## Adding a Bookmark

1. Touch the Menu button.

2. Touch Save to Bookmarks.

3. Change the bookmark name if you want to. It defaults to the web page's title.

4. Edit the web page link if you want to or leave it as is (normally best).

5. Select the account to save the bookmark under. You can choose one of your Google accounts or Local.

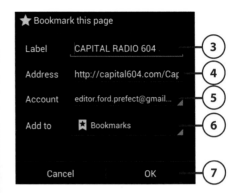

## Where to Save Bookmarks

When you save bookmarks, you can choose to save them locally or to one of your Google accounts. If you choose to save a bookmark locally, it is only saved to your Galaxy Nexus. The bookmark is not synchronized to the Google cloud or made available anywhere other than on your phone. If you choose to save the bookmark to one of your Google accounts, that bookmark is stored in the Google cloud and is then available to you on any device where you use that same Google account. This includes when you log in to your Google account on your desktop computer, and any Android smartphone or tablet that you purchase and use in the future.

6. Choose where to save the bookmark. You can choose the Bookmarks folder, Other folder, or Home screen.

7. Touch OK.

# Browsing History

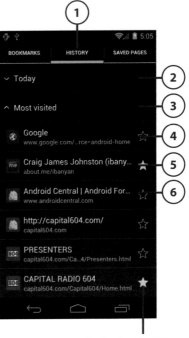

1. Touch History.

2. Touch to expand web history by day/date.

3. Touch to see your most-visited websites of all time.

4. Touch the open star to bookmark the web page.

5. Touch the closed star to remove the bookmark from the web page.

6. Touch and hold a web page to see more options.

7. Touch to open the bookmark in the current browser tab.

8. Touch to open the bookmark in a new browser tab.

9. Touch to save the web page as a bookmark.

10. Touch to share the link using varies methods including email, Twitter, and Facebook.

11. Touch to copy the link to the clipboard. After it is in the clipboard, you can paste it into any other screen, such as the body of an email message.

12. Touch to remove the web page from your browser's history.

13. Touch to set the bookmark as the home page of the web browser. The home page is always loaded when you start the web browser.

**Indicates that the web page is bookmarked**

## Saved Pages

1. Touch Saved Pages.

2. Touch a saved page to view it.

3. Touch and hold a saved page, and then touch Delete Saved Page to delete it.

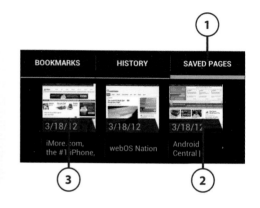

### Go Live

While you are viewing saved web pages, you are not able to touch any of the links on the page. This is because the saved page is simply a screen shot of the web page that you can zoom in on and move around. If you enter an area where you are again getting cellular or Wi-Fi coverage, you can take the page live again by touching the Menu button and touching Go Live.

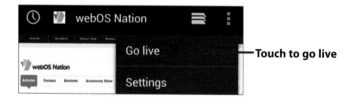

Touch to go live

# Managing Multiple Tabs

Your Galaxy Nexus can have multiple web pages open at one time, each in a different tab. This enables you to work with multiple websites at once and switch between them. Here is how to open and work with multiple tabs.

1. Touch the tab icon.

2. Touch to add a new Browser tab.

3. Touch to close a Browser tab.

4. Touch a tab to switch to it.

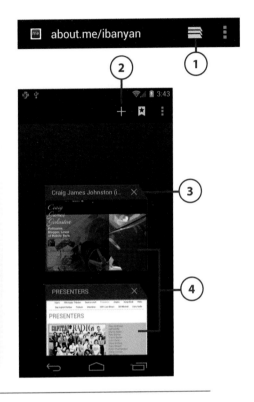

## Browse in Secret

If you want to visit a website in secret, you can. Visiting a website in secret means that the site you visit does not appear in your browser history or search history and does not otherwise leave a trace of itself on your Galaxy Nexus. To do this you must create a new Incognito browser tab. Inside that browser tab, all sites you visit are in secret. To create a new Incognito browser tab, while in the browser tab screen, touch the Menu button and touch New Incognito Tab.

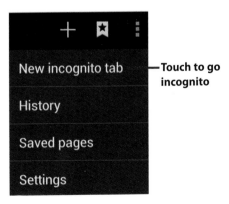

Touch to go incognito

# Customizing Browser Settings

Your Galaxy Nexus browser is customizable. Here are the different settings you can adjust.

1. Touch the Menu button.

2. Touch Settings.

3. Touch General.

4. Touch to set the current web page as the browser home page.

5. Touch the check box to have the web browser automatically fill in fields in web forms.

6. Touch to enter the information that will be automatically entered into web forms.

7. Touch to return to the main Settings screen.

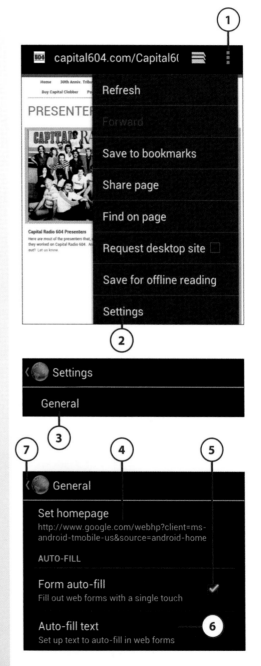

**8.** Touch Privacy & Security.

**9.** Touch to clear Browser's cache. The cache is used to store data and images from websites you visit so that the next time you go back, some of the web page can be loaded straight out of memory.

**10.** Touch to clear Browser's history. This clears the history of websites you have visited on your Galaxy Nexus.

**11.** Touch to enable or disable website security warnings. Your Galaxy Nexus can warn you if a website you are visiting appears to have a security violation of some kind.

**12.** Touch Accept Cookies to enable or disable accepting cookies. Browser cookies are used by websites to personalize your visit by storing information specific to you in the cookies.

**13.** Touch to clear all cookies from your Galaxy Nexus.

**14.** Touch to enable or disable the feature where the browser remembers information that you enter in forms on websites.

**15.** Scroll down to see more settings.

**16.** Touch to clear any form data that the browser has remembered.

**17.** Touch Enable Location to enable or disable the ability for websites to access your GPS information.

**18.** Touch to clear location settings for all websites you have visited.

**19.** Touch Remember Passwords to enable or disable Browser's ability to remember the usernames and passwords you enter on different websites.

**20.** Touch to clear any passwords you have previously entered while on websites.

**21.** Touch to return to the Settings main screen.

**22.** Touch Accessibility.

**23.** Touch to enable or disable the ability of your Galaxy Nexus to always allow you to zoom in on websites even if the websites attempt to restrict zooming.

**24.** Use the slider to adjust the text scaling.

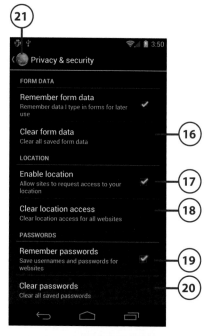

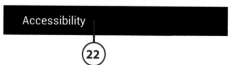

## What Is Text Scaling?

When you use text scaling, you instruct your Galaxy Nexus to always increase or decrease the font sizes used on a web page by a specific percentage. For example, you can automatically make all text 150% larger than was originally intended.

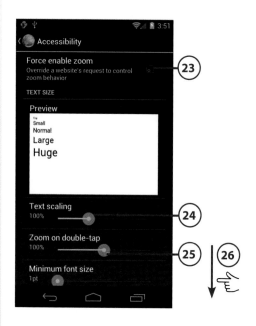

**25.** Use the slider to adjust how much a web page zooms in when you double-tap.

**26.** Scroll down for more settings.

**27.** Use the slider to adjust the minimum font size used no matter what the web page requires.

**28.** Touch to enable or disable inverted web page rendering.

**29.** Use the slider to adjust the contrast of the rendered web page if inverted rendering is enabled.

## Why Inverted Rendering?

When you enable inverted rendering, your Galaxy Nexus automatically flips the colors white and black, but it also converts all other colors to grayscale. Using inverted rendering can help some people with vision impairments to see web pages more effectively.

**30.** Touch to return to the main Settings screen.

**31.** Touch Advanced.

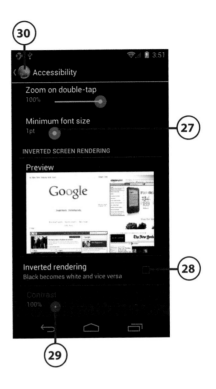

32. Touch to select the search engine used when you type in search terms. Your choices are Google, Yahoo!, and Bing.

33. Touch to enable or disable force loading a new tab in the background. When this is enabled, a new tab does not automatically become the current tab; you have to switch to it to make it the current tab.

34. Touch to enable or disable JavaScript. JavaScript is used on many web pages for formatting and other functions, so you might want to leave this enabled.

35. Touch to enable or disable plug-ins. Plug-ins enhance the standard functionality of Browser.

36. Touch to see which websites have information stored on your Galaxy Nexus and choose to clear that information.

37. Touch to change the default zoom level when opening web pages. Choices are Far, Medium, and Close. The default zoom is Medium.

38. Touch to enable or disable page overview. Page overview is when a page appears zoomed out to an overview of the page, as opposed to the page being viewed at 100% zoom.

39. Scroll down for more settings.

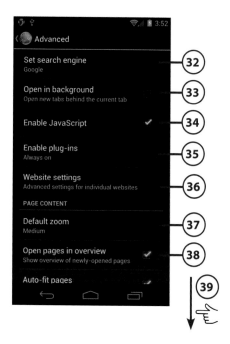

**40.** Touch to enable or disable making web pages automatically fit the screen horizontally.

**41.** Touch to block pop-up windows. Pop-up windows are almost always advertisements, so keeping this enabled is a good idea; however, some websites might require that you turn off pop-up blocking.

## How Does Pop-Up Blocking Work?

When you enable pop-up blocking, your Galaxy Nexus automatically blocks any website request to pop up a window. This is good because almost every pop-up on a website is some kind of scam to get you to touch a link in that pop-up window, taking you to a new site. Sometimes, though, pop-ups are legitimate, and a website that needs you to allow pop-ups will ask you to allow them. You can disable the pop-up blocker anytime and then re-enable it when you stop using that website. Unlike desktop computers, you cannot temporarily stop blocking pop-ups, so you need to remember to manually disable and enable the pop-up blocker.

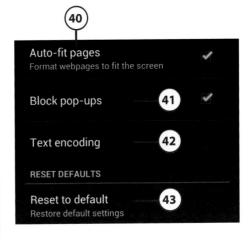

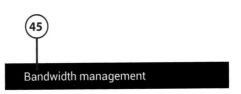

**42.** Touch Text Encoding to choose a different encoding option. Use this to select text encoding for Japanese and other characters.

**43.** Touch Reset to Default to return Browser to the out-of-the-box state and clear all Browser data.

**44.** Touch to return to the main Settings screen.

**45.** Touch Bandwidth Management.

**46.** Touch to control search result preloading. You can set this Never, Only on WiFi, or Always.

## What Is Result Preloading?

Result preloading is an option that allows your Galaxy Nexus to predict which links on a web page you are likely to click, and then preload the web page that the link points to into memory. If it has predicted correctly and loaded the correct pages into memory, when you touch a link, that page renders straight from the memory of your Galaxy Nexus instead of first loading over the network. Although this can be a time saver, it means that your Galaxy Nexus might be preloading pages that you will not look at, which can lead to wasted data usage. When you enable result preloading, you can choose Only on WiFi, which tells your Galaxy Nexus to automatically enable this feature only when you are connected to a Wi-Fi network; the feature is disabled when you are on a cellular data connection.

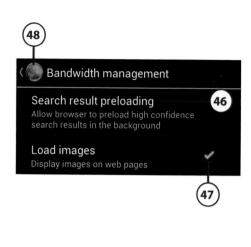

**47.** Touch Load Images to enable or disable image loading. When Load Images is disabled, Browser loads web pages with no images, which makes the pages load faster.

**48.** Touch to return to the main Settings screen.

**49.** Touch Labs.

**50.** Touch to enable or disable Quick Controls.

**51.** Touch to enable or disable Fullscreen mode. In this mode, the Notification Bar at the top of the screen along with the clock and network indicators is hidden to give you that little extra space to view the web page.

**52.** Touch to return to the main Settings screen.

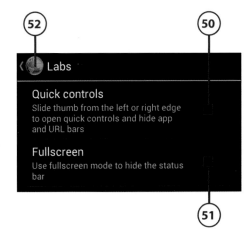

## What Is Quick Controls?

If you enable Quick Controls, when you browse a website the address bar at the top of the screen is hidden to give you a little extra screen space for browsing. To continue to use the menus and functions that are now hidden, drag your thumb in from the left or right of the screen. The Quick Controls appear around your thumb.

**Drag your thumb to see the Quick Controls**

Touch to call
the sender

Touch to play
the video

In this chapter, you learn how to work with text and multimedia messages. Topics include the following:

→ Creating text and multimedia messages

→ Attaching files to multimedia messages

→ Saving received multimedia attachments

→ Working with text messages on your SIM card

# Text and Multimedia Messaging

Short Message Service (SMS), also known as text messaging, has been around for a long time and is still used today as the primary form of communication for many younger phone users. Multimedia Message Service (MMS) is a newer form of text messaging that can contain pictures, audio, and video. Your Galaxy Nexus can work with both SMS and MMS, but both are called text messaging.

## Messaging Application

The Messaging application is what you use to send and receive text messages. This application has all the features you need to compose, send, receive, and manage these messages. Let's take a look.

1. Touch the Messaging icon on the Home screen.

2. Touch to compose a new text message.

3. Touch the sender's picture to show the Quick Contact bar.

4. Touch a message thread to open it.

5. Touch the Menu button to change the Messaging app settings or to delete all messages.

6. Indicates how many unread messages there are in all message threads.

7. Indicates how many messages there are in a message thread.

8. Touch to search for a text message.

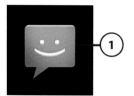

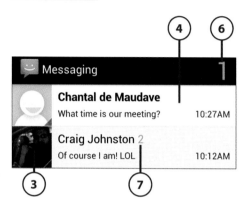

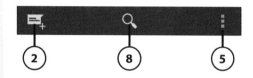

## Managing Settings

You manage how your SMS and MMS messages are handled through the settings of the Messaging application. Before we actually start working with SMS and MMS, let's take a look at the settings.

1. Touch the Menu button.

2. Touch Settings.

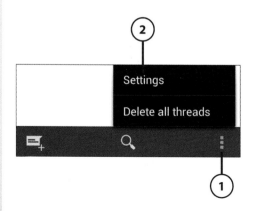

**3.** Touch to enable or disable automatically deleting old messages when the limits you set in steps 4 and 5 are reached.

**4.** Touch to change the text message limit per thread (or conversation). The maximum number you can type is 999. When the limit is reached, messages within the thread or conversation are deleted using the first in, first out (FIFO) method.

**5.** Touch to change the multimedia message limit per thread (or conversation). The maximum number you can type is 999. When the limit is reached, messages within the thread or conversation are deleted using the first in, first out (FIFO) method.

**6.** Touch to enable or disable delivery reports for SMS or text messages that you send.

## Delivery Reports

When you enable delivery reports and send a text message, your Galaxy Nexus keeps track of the message and provides confirmation that it was successfully delivered to the recipient(s).

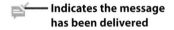 **Indicates the message has been delivered**

**7.** Touch to manage messages that might still be on your SIM card. See the "Managing Messages on Your SIM Card" section later in this chapter for more information.

**8.** Touch to enable or disable delivery reports for MMS or multimedia messages that you send.

**9.** Scroll down for more settings.

**10.** Touch to enable or disable read reports. This feature, while supported on your Galaxy Nexus, is not well-supported by other phones, so you might not get read reports from some recipients.

**11.** Touch to enable or disable automatically retrieving multimedia messages.

**12.** Touch to enable or disable automatically retrieving multimedia messages while roaming.

**13.** Touch to enable or disable receiving a notification that a new text message has arrived. The notification is displayed in the status bar.

**14.** Touch to choose a different ringtone to be played when new text message arrives.

**15.** Touch to enable or disable vibration when new messages are received.

**16.** Touch to save your changes and return to the main Messaging screen.

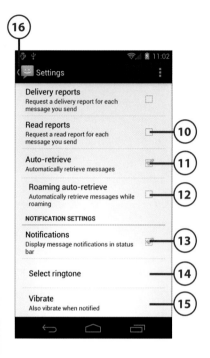

## Don't Auto-Retrieve MMS While Roaming

The reason its best to leave auto-retrieval of multimedia messages disabled when you travel to other countries is because auto-retrieving messages when you're roaming can result in a big bill from your provider. International carriers love to charge large amounts of money for people traveling to their countries and using their networks. The only time it is a good idea to leave this enabled is if your carrier offers an international SMS or MMS bundle where you pay a flat rate upfront before leaving. When you have auto-retrieve disabled, you see a Download button next to a multimedia message. You have to touch it to manually download the message.

| | |
|---|---|
| &lt;Subject: no subject&gt;<br>Message size: 214KB<br>Expires: Mar 27 | Download ——**Touch to manually retrieve the message** |

## Composing Messages

When you compose a new message, you do not need to make a conscious decision whether it is an SMS or MMS message. As soon as you add a subject line or attach a file to your message, your Galaxy Nexus automatically treats the message as an MMS. Here is how to compose and send messages.

1. Touch to compose a new message.

2. Start typing the phone number of the recipient, or if the person is in your contacts, type the name. If the name is found, touch the mobile number.

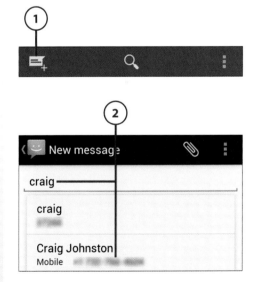

3. Touch to start typing your message.

4. Touch to send your message.

Touch to attach a file

Touch to speak your message instead of typing it

## Insert Smiley Icons

There are two ways to insert smiley icons (or emoticons). The quick way is to touch the smiley icon on the keyboard. If you touch it just once, you insert a smiling face icon. If you touch and hold it, you can then choose from a range of emotions. The second way to insert a smiley icon is to touch the Menu button and touch Insert Smiley.

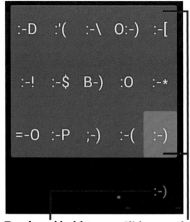

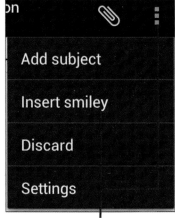

Touch and hold to reveal all smileys

Slide over the smiley you want and release your finger

Touch to choose a smiley

## MESSAGE LIMITS AND MESSAGES

Text messages can only be 163 characters long. To get around this limit, most modern phones simply break up text messages you type into 163-character chunks. On your Galaxy Nexus, you can see the number of characters you have typed; when you have typed 163 or more characters, you can see the number of text messages your Galaxy Nexus will send. The phone receiving the message simply combines them all together into one message. This is important to know if your wireless plan has a text message limit. When you create one text message, your Galaxy Nexus might actually break the message into two or more.

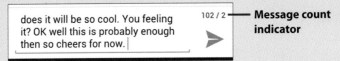

**Message count indicator**

# Attaching Files to Messages

If you want to send a picture, audio file, or video along with your text message, all you need to do is attach the file. Attaching a file turns your SMS message into an MMS message.

1. Touch to attach a file.

2. Touch to attach a picture already stored in your Gallery app.

3. Touch to take a picture and attach it.

4. Touch to attach a video already stored in your Gallery app.

5. Touch to capture a video and attach it.

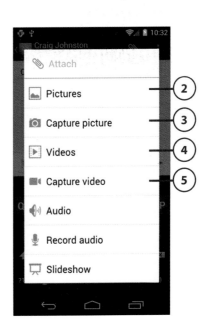

6. Touch to attach an audio file that is already stored on your Galaxy Nexus.

7. Touch to record audio and attach it.

8. Touch to attach a slideshow that is already stored on your Galaxy Nexus.

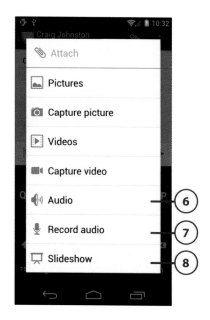

## It's Not All Good

**Is It Worth Attaching?**

Attaching files to text messages is not as useful as you think. Most carriers limit the attachment size to around 300KB. This means that you can only really attach about 60 seconds of very, very low-quality video, small pictures with the dimensions of 640 × 480 (VGA size), and very short audio files. To make matters worse, the Messaging app does not have any built-in way of compressing attachments. If you are attaching previously taken pictures, you can only attach pictures that were taken with the Camera app set to VGA (which is 640 × 480). If you are attaching prerecorded video, there is no way to set the Camera app to record low-quality video, so nothing you've previously recorded will be small enough unless you have saved a video someone else sent you via text message. Choosing the option of capturing pictures, capturing video, or recording audio when you choose to attach is the only way you can guarantee that the files are small enough. This is because when you do this, the camera and audio recorder apps are set to a mode that makes them record low-quality audio and take low-quality pictures.

# Receiving Messages

When you receive a new SMS or MMS, you can read the message, view attachments, and even save the attachments onto your Galaxy Nexus.

1. When a new SMS or MMS arrives, you are notified with a ringtone. A notification also displays in the status bar.

2. Pull down the status bar to see newly arrived messages.

3. Touch a message alert to open it.

4. Touch an attachment to open it.

5. Touch and hold a message to reveal more options. Skip to step 7 for more about the additional options.

6. Touch to compose a reply to the message.

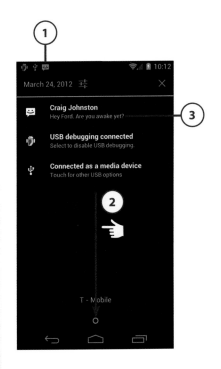

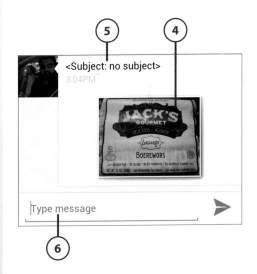

**7.** Touch to forward the message.

**8.** Touch to save the attachment.

**9.** Touch to prevent a message from being deleted when the thread message limit is reached. Read more about message limits in the "Managing Settings" section earlier in this chapter.

**10.** Touch to view details about the message.

**11.** Touch to delete the message. This deletes just the message and not the entire thread.

### Usable Content

If a text message contains links to websites, phone numbers, or email addresses, touching those links results in the appropriate action being initiated. For example, when you touch a phone number your Galaxy Nexus calls the number; when you touch a web link, the Galaxy Nexus opens the page in Browser.

## Managing Messages on Your SIM Card

Many old cell phones store text messages on the SIM card and not in the phone's memory. If you have just upgraded from an older phone you might still have text messages on the SIM card that you would like to retrieve. Here is how.

**1.** Touch the Menu button while on the main Messaging app screen.

**2.** Touch Settings.

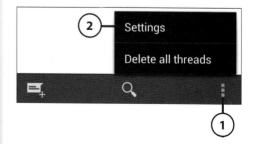

3. Touch Manage SIM card messages.

4. Touch and hold on a message.

5. Touch to copy the message to the phone memory.

6. Touch to delete the message.

7. Touch and hold the sender's picture.

8. Touch to add the sender's number to your contacts.

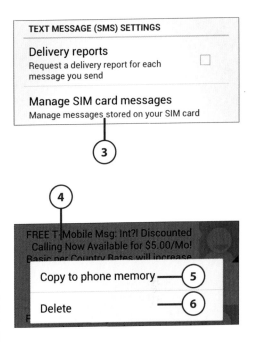

Touch and hold to
activate bedside
mode

In this chapter, you learn how to set the time, use the Clock application, and use the Calendar application. Topics include the following:

→ Synchronizing to the correct time
→ Working with the Clock application
→ Setting alarms
→ Working with the Calendar

# Working with Date, Time, and Calendar

Your Galaxy Nexus has a Clock application that you can use as a bedside alarm. The Calendar application synchronizes to your Google or Microsoft Exchange Calendars and enables you to create meetings while on the road and to always know where your next meeting is.

## Setting the Date and Time

Before you start working with the Clock and Calendar applications, you need to make sure that your Galaxy Nexus has the correct date and time.

1. Touch Settings.

2. Touch Date & Time.

3. Touch to enable or disable synchronizing time and date with the wireless carrier. It is best to leave this enabled as it automatically sets date and time based on where you are travelling.

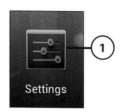

## Does Network Time Sync Always Work?

In some countries, on some carriers, time synchronization does not work. This means that when you get off the plane and turn Airplane Mode off, after a reasonable amount of time the time, date, and time zone will still be incorrect. In these instances, it is best to disable the Automatic Date & Time option and manually set the time, date, and time zone yourself. You can try it on automatic in the next country you visit or when you are back in your home country.

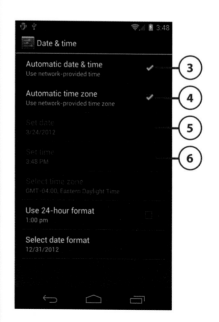

4. Touch to enable or disable synchronizing the time zone with the wireless carrier. It is best to leave this enabled as it automatically sets the time zone based on where you are travelling.

5. Touch to set the date if you choose to disable network synchronization.

6. Touch to set the time if you choose to disable network synchronization.

7. Touch to set the time zone if you choose to disable network synchronization.

8. Touch to enable or disable the use of 24-hour time format. This makes your Galaxy Nexus represent time without a.m. or p.m. For example 1:00 p.m. becomes 13:00.

9. Touch to change the way in which the date is represented. For example in the U.S. we normally write the date with the month first (12/31/2012). You can make your Galaxy Nexus display the date with day first (31/12/2012) or with the year first (2012/12/31).

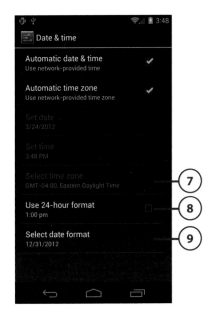

# Clock Application

The Clock application is preinstalled on your Galaxy Nexus and provides the functionality of a bedside clock and alarm clock.

## Navigating the Clock Application

1. Touch the Clock icon.

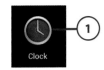

2. Touch to set or edit alarms.

3. Rotate your Galaxy Nexus onto its side to increase the size of the digits.

4. Touch the screen briefly to dim the brightness of the screen.

5. Touch and hold the screen to activate the blue digits.

## Trick to Activate Blue Digits and Dim the Screen

Although it is not obvious how to do it, you can dim the Clock app and show the blue digits at the same time. To do this you must follow a specific sequence. First, touch the screen briefly to dim the brightness. Next touch and hold the screen to activate the blue digits.

# Managing Alarms

The Clock application enables you to set multiple alarms. These can be one-time alarms or recurring alarms. Even if you exit the Clock application, the alarms you set still trigger.

1. Touch to manage alarms and show clock preferences.

2. Touch an existing alarm to edit it.

3. Touch to enable or disable an existing alarm.

4. Touch to return to the clock view.

5. Touch to add a new alarm.

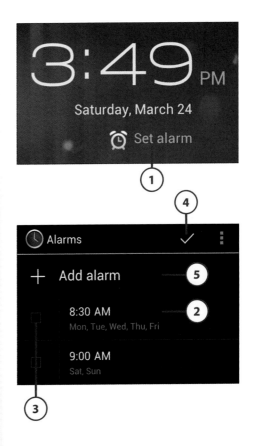

# Adding or Editing an Alarm

The steps we follow to add an alarm are the same for editing an existing alarm.

1. Touch to add a new alarm or touch to edit an existing alarm.

2. Touch to enable or disable the alarm.

3. Touch to set the time the alarm must trigger.

4. Touch to set if your alarm must repeat and which days of the week to repeat. This is useful for example, if you want an alarm to wake you on week days but not weekend days.

5. Touch to choose a ringtone to play when the alarm triggers.

6. Touch to enable or disable vibrating in addition to playing the ringtone when the alarm triggers.

7. Touch to add a title for your alarm. For example you could call it "Wake up."

8. Touch OK to save your changes.

Touch to cancel any changes   Touch to delete an existing alarm

## Clock Settings

Use the Settings to control how all alarms function.

1. Touch the Menu button.

2. Touch Settings.

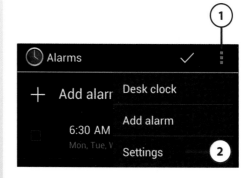

3. Touch to enable or disable playing the alarm even if your Galaxy Nexus is in silent mode.

4. Touch to set the volume for all alarms.

5. Touch to set the duration of the snooze period. Your choices range between 5 and 30 minutes.

6. Touch to set how long the alarm plays before it automatically silences itself. Your choices range from 5 minutes to 30 minutes; alternatively you can set it to off so that the alarm plays until you wake up and dismiss it.

7. Touch to set how the volume buttons behave if you press either of them when the alarm sounds. Your choices are Snooze and Dismiss.

8. Touch to set the default ringtone for all alarms.

9. Touch to save the settings and return to the Clock main screen.

# Using the Calendar Application

The Calendar application enables you to synchronize all of your calendars from Google, your work account, and other online calendars. You can accept appointments and create and modify appointments right on your phone. Any changes are automatically synchronized wirelessly back to your Google, work, or other online calendars in real time.

# The Calendar Main Screen

The main screen of the Calendar app shows a one-day, one-week, or one-month view of your appointments. The Calendar app also shows events from multiple calendars at the same time.

1. Touch the Calendar icon.

2. Swipe left to go backward in time.

3. Swipe right to go forward in time.

4. Touch to show today's date.

5. Touch to choose the calendar view. You can choose from the month, week, day, and agenda views.

6. Touch the Menu button for Calendar app actions.

7. Touch to search the calendar for an event.

8. Touch to create a new event.

9. Touch to manually refresh the calendar view.

10. Touch to choose which calendars to display and which ones to synchronize.

11. Touch to change the Calendar app settings.

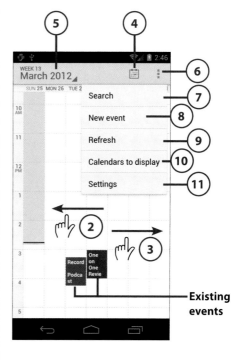

## Event Colors

The Calendar app can display one calendar or many calendars at the same time. If you choose to display multiple calendars, events from each calendar are color coded so you can tell which events are from which calendar.

# Choosing Which Calendars to View

You can choose which calendars the Calendar app shows at the same time and select which calendars you want to synchronize to your Galaxy Nexus.

1. Touch the Menu button.

2. Touch Calendars to Display.

3. Select which calendars you want to synchronize to your Galaxy Nexus

4. Touch to choose which calendars to synchronize to your Galaxy Nexus.

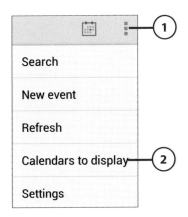

Search

New event

Refresh

Calendars to display

Settings

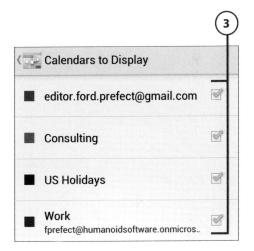

Calendars to Display

editor.ford.prefect@gmail.com

Consulting

US Holidays

Work
fprefect@humanoidsoftware.onmicros..

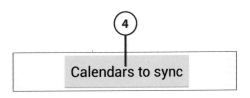

Calendars to sync

5. Touch an account to expand its list of calendars.

6. Select which calendars you want to synchronize to your Galaxy Nexus. Note that some kinds of accounts (such as Google) allow multiple calendars per account, which is why you see Consulting and US Holidays under the Google account in this example.

7. Touch OK to save your changes and return to the Calendar select view.

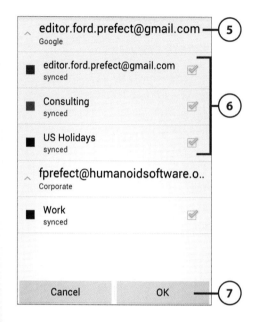

# Calendar Settings

1. Touch the Menu button.

2. Touch Settings.

3. Touch General Preferences.

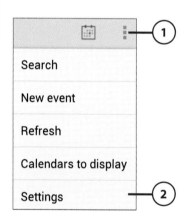

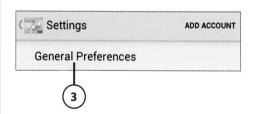

4. Touch to enable or disable hiding events that you have declined.

5. Touch to enable or disable showing the week number. For example, March 26th is in week 13.

6. Touch to set the first day of your week. You can choose Saturday, Sunday, or Monday. You can also choose Locale Default, which allows the locale you have set in the device settings to determine what the first day of the week is. Please see Chapter 11, "Customizing Your Galaxy Nexus," for more information on setting the device locale.

7. Touch to enable or disable using your home time zone when displaying the calendar and event times. When this is enabled, your home time zone is always used even when you are not travelling in it.

8. Touch to set your home time zone if you enabled Use Home Time Zone in step 7.

9. Touch to clear any calendar searches that you have previously performed.

10. Scroll down for more settings.

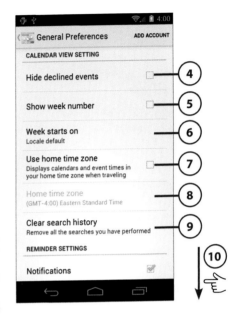

11. Touch to enable or disable notifications for calendar events.

12. Touch to choose the ringtone to play when you are being alerted for calendar events.

13. Touch to choose whether your Galaxy Nexus should also vibrate when the event ringtone plays.

14. Touch to enable or disable a pop-up notification to also be displayed when you are being notified of a calendar event. This pop-up window displays over any app that you are currently using.

15. Touch to set the default event reminder time.

16. Touch to return to the main settings screen.

17. Touch an account to choose which of its calendars synchronize to your Galaxy Nexus.

18. Touch to save your settings and return to the main Calendar screen.

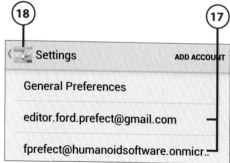

# Adding a New Event

While you're on the road you can add a new appointment or event, and you can even invite people to it. Events you add synchronize to your Google and corporate calendars in real time.

1. Touch the Menu button.

2. Touch New Event.

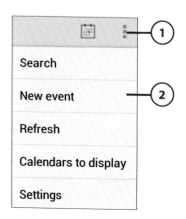

## Quicker Way to Add an Event

Instead of adding a new event via the Menu button, you can touch on the day you want to create the event and the time of day you want to create it.

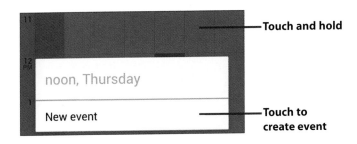

**Touch and hold**

noon, Thursday

New event

**Touch to create event**

**3.** Touch to select which calendar to add the event to.

**4.** Touch to enter a title for your event.

**5.** Enter where the event will take place. This can be a full physical address, which is useful because most smartphones can map the address.

**6.** Touch to select the start date and time of the event.

**7.** Touch to select the end date and time of the event.

**8.** Touch to mark the event as an all-day event.

**9.** Touch to select the time zone the meeting will be held in. This is useful if you will be travelling to the meeting in a different time zone.

**10.** Enter the event guests, or event invitees. As you type names, your Galaxy Nexus retrieves matching names from your Contacts and your corporate directory.

11. Enter a description for the event.

12. Scroll down to set more event settings.

13. Touch to set this as a recurring event. You can make it repeat daily, weekly, or monthly, but you can also set a meeting to repeat—for example, monthly but only every last Thursday.

14. Touch to set how many minutes before the event you are reminded.

15. Touch to set how you are reminded. You can choose to be notified on the device like all other notifications or via email.

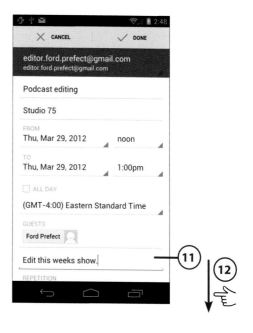

## Recurring Events Are Not Flexible

Unfortunately when you choose to make an event repeat the choices you are given are not flexible. For example if you want to set up an event that repeats every Thursday, you cannot do this unless you create the event on a Thursday. Let's hope that this is addressed in a future release of Android.

16. Touch to remove a reminder.

17. Touch to add an additional reminder.

18. Touch to choose how to show your availability during this event. You can choose Busy or Available.

19. Touch to choose the privacy of the event. You can choose Public or make it private so only you can see it. If the event is being created on your corporate calendar, setting it to Private means that people can see you are busy but cannot see the event details.

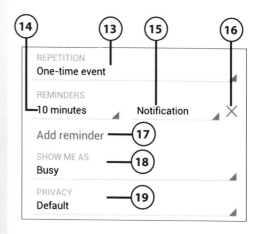

**20.** Touch to save the event. Any attendees that you have added will automatically be sent an event invitation.

## Edit and Delete an Event

To edit or delete a calendar event, touch the event and either edit it by touching the pencil icon or delete the event by touching the trash can icon. When you successfully delete an event, the Calendar application sends an event decline notice to the event organizer. You don't have to first decline the meeting before deleting it because this is all taken care of automatically.

# Responding to a Gmail Event Invitation

When you are invited to an event, you can choose your response right on your Galaxy Nexus.

**1.** Touch to open the event invitation email.

**2.** Touch Yes, Maybe, or No to indicate whether you will be attending.

3. Touch the event location to have it mapped in Google Maps or another mapping app that you may have installed (such as Google Earth).

4. Change your event response if you need to.

5. Touch to remove an event reminder.

6. Touch to add an additional event reminder.

7. Touch to save your changes.

## Alternative Event Respond Method

You can also respond to Gmail and corporate event invitations directly in the Calendar app. When you receive an event invite in Gmail, it appears in your calendar with an outline. Touch the outlined event to open it and respond. If you receive an event invite in your corporate calendar, it is automatically inserted into the calendar but set as tentative. Touch the event to accept or decline it. One word of caution: Gmail does not synchronize the calendar view in real time, so it might take a few minutes for the new event to appear, although your Gmail emails arrive in real time. Using Gmail might still be the fastest way of responding to Google invites.

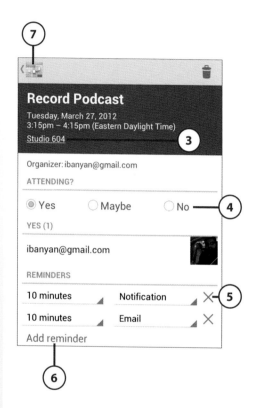

# Responding to a Corporate Event Invitation

When someone invites you to a new event, you receive an email in your corporate inbox with the details of that meeting.

1. Touch to open the event invitation.

2. Touch Invite to see the invitation itself.

3. Touch to view the event invite in the calendar view. This is useful if you want to make sure you don't have a conflict.

4. Touch to choose your response.

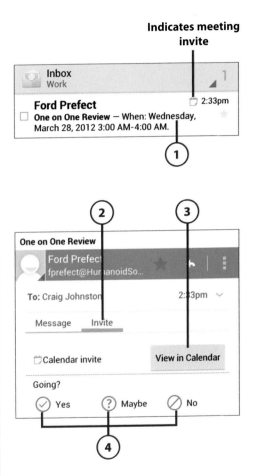

**Indicates meeting invite**

Face recognition

In this chapter, you learn how to take pictures with your Galaxy Nexus, how to store them, and how to share them with friends. Topics include the following:

- → Using the camera
- → Taking panoramic pictures
- → Sharing pictures
- → Synchronizing pictures
- → Viewing pictures

# Taking, Storing, and Viewing Pictures

Your Galaxy Nexus has a decent 5-megapixel camera with mechanical auto-focus. This means it can take really good pictures. After you take those great pictures, you can share them with friends. You can also synchronize the pictures directly with your computer or use Google Photos in the cloud.

## Using the Camera

Let's start by looking at the Camera application itself before we discuss sharing pictures with friends or synchronizing them with your computer.

1. Touch to launch the Camera.

2. Touch to change the camera mode between still camera, panoramic camera, and video camera

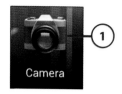

Camera

3. Touch to switch between the front-facing camera and the rear-facing camera.

4. Touch to change the camera settings. (See the next section for more information about the camera settings.)

5. Slide up and down to zoom in and out.

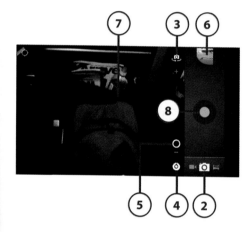

6. Touch to review pictures in the Gallery application. See more about reviewing, sharing, and editing pictures in the Gallery application for your Galaxy Nexus later in this chapter.

7. Touch anywhere in the frame to make the camera focus specifically in the area. The focus box turns green if it's successful and red if it cannot focus.

8. Touch to take a picture.

# Camera Settings

Using camera settings you can change things such as the resolution of each picture, picture review time, and more.

1. Touch to reveal the camera settings.

2. Touch to set the camera flash mode. The camera flash mode setting is only visible when you have the rear-facing camera selected.

3. Select either Auto (which lets the camera decide when to fire the flash), On (which means the flash is always used), or Off (when means the flash is never used).

4. Touch to set the White Balance

5. Select either Auto (which lets the camera decide on the White Balance setting) or choose specific lighting conditions.

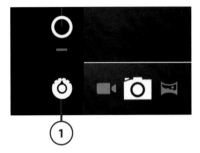

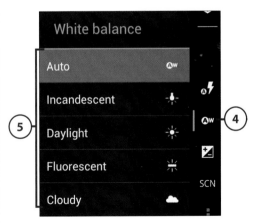

6. Touch to change the exposure setting, which enables you to force the camera to either under-expose or overexpose a picture.

7. Choose positive numbers to overexpose the picture (keep the shutter open longer) or negative numbers to underexpose the pic-ture (keep the shutter open for a shorter period).

8. Touch to change the scene mode. Changing the scene can help the camera adjust itself to the type of scenery and type of picture being taken.

9. Choose a scene like Action or Night, or leave the mode on Auto to let the camera decide.

10. Touch the Menu button to see more settings.

11. Touch the arrows to adjust the resolution of the picture. The highest is 5 megapixels for the rear-facing camera and 1.3 mega-pixels for the front-facing camera.

12. Touch to enable or disable storing your geographic location in the picture or video.

13. Touch to restore all camera set-tings to their out-of-the-box, fac-tory settings.

14. Touch to close the camera set-tings.

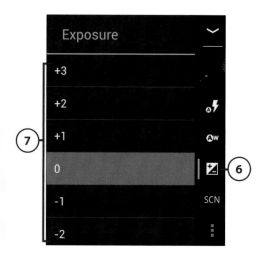

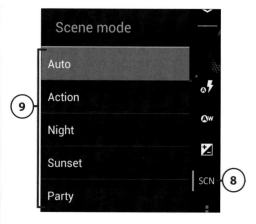

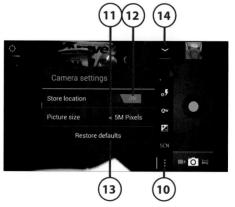

## Why Change the Image Resolution?

Step 11 describes how you can change the resolution of images captured by the camera. As a rule of thumb, you always want to capture images at the highest resolution possible. This is because you want to capture the moment in the best clarity you can, even if you later edit a copy of the image to make it smaller. One reason you might want to lower the resolution of the captured images is to send those specific images to people using text messaging. Chapter 7, "Text and Multimedia Messaging," explains that the messaging app does not automatically reduce the size of images you want to send in the same way that many other phones do. This means that you have to plan ahead and decide what images you want to send via text messaging, and reduce the resolution of these images.

# Taking Regular Pictures

Now that you have the settings the way you want them, take a few pictures. You can jump straight to step 5 and take the picture, but you might want to first set up your shot. Remember to always take pictures in landscape mode for the best results.

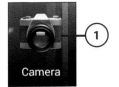

1. Touch the Camera icon.

2. Touch to switch between the front-facing or rear-facing camera.

3. Slide up and down to zoom in and zoom out.

4. Touch the area of the frame you want to focus on specifically. When you release your finger, the camera indicates a green focus box if it can successfully focus or a red focus box if it cannot.

5. Touch to take the picture.

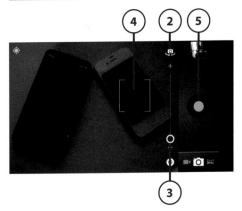

## Focus on Parts of a Picture

With the Galaxy Nexus, you can actually focus on a certain part of a picture. By touching the part of the picture you want in focus, you see that the rest of the picture goes out of focus. Using this trick enables you to take some amazing pictures.

# Taking Panoramic Pictures

Your Galaxy Nexus can take panoramic pictures. Panoramic pictures are achieved by taking multiple pictures from left to right or right to left, and stitching them together in one long picture. Luckily your Galaxy Nexus does all that work for you.

1. Touch the Camera icon.

2. Touch to change the camera mode.

3. Touch to select Panoramic.

4. Touch to start the panorama.

5. Slowly rotate your body from left to right or right to left to capture the panorama. Use the indicator at the bottom of the screen to track your progress.

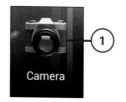

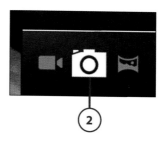

**Indicates your progress**

6. When you have rotated all the way, the camera automatically stitches the pictures together into a panorama and saves it.

**Indicates saving progress**

## Can You Change the Length of the Panorama?

To create shorter panoramas, instead of rotating all the way from left to right or right to left until the indicator at the bottom of the screen reaches the opposite end, you can touch the green button to immediately stop the panorama process and save it as is. This enables you to create shorter panoramic pictures.

## Moving Too Fast

When you take Panoramic pictures, you have to rotate slowly. If you start moving too fast, the camera indicates this to you by changing the progress indicator to red and putting a red border around the picture. Slow down when this happens; otherwise the panorama will not look good.

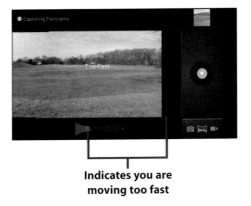

**Indicates you are moving too fast**

# Viewing and Managing Your Photos

No matter if you have snapped pictures using your Galaxy Nexus or have synchronized photos from a computer, you can use the Gallery application to manage, edit, and share your photos.

## Navigating the Gallery

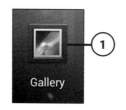

1. Touch to launch the Gallery application.

2. Touch a thumbnail photo to open an album.

3. Touch to reorder the way the photos are displayed. Instead of displaying them by the album they are in, you can display photos grouped by locations, times, people, and tags.

4. Swipe left and right to see all photo albums.

5. Touch to launch the Camera app.

6. Touch the photos labeled as Camera to see pictures taken on your Galaxy Nexus.

7. Touch the Menu button to see Gallery app actions.

8. Touch to choose which photos are available offline. See more about moving photos offline later in this chapter.

9. Touch to manually refresh the Gallery view. This is helpful to update the view after very recently uploading photos to Google from your computer.

10. Touch to change the Gallery app settings.

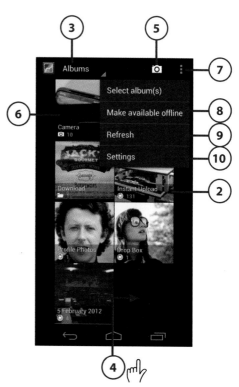

# Deleting Photo Albums

You can delete one or many photo albums, but only if they were created on your Galaxy Nexus. Albums created on your desktop computer that you can also see on your Galaxy Nexus cannot be deleted.

1. Touch and hold a photo album.

2. Touch to select additional albums if you want to.

3. Touch the Menu button.

4. Touch Delete.

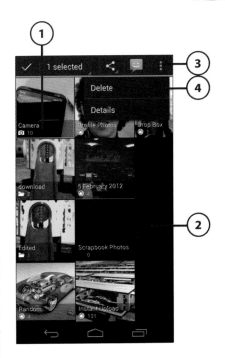

# Open a Photo Album

After you open a photo album, you can manage the photos in it, edit them, and share them.

1. Touch an album to see all pictures in it.

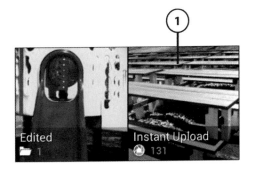

2. Touch to see a slide show of all the photos in the album.

3. Touch the Menu button and then Group By to group the photos by location, time, people, and tags.

4. Touch a photo to view it.

5. Touch to return to the main Gallery app screen.

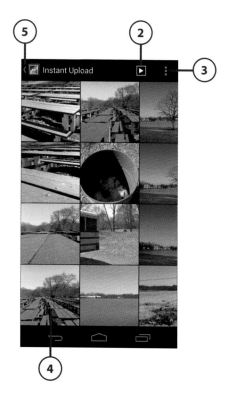

# Reviewing and Sharing Pictures

After you open a photo you can review it and share it with your friends.

1. Double-tap the picture to zoom in to the maximum zoom level. Double-tap again to zoom all the way back to 100%.

2. Use the pinch gesture to have a more controlled zoom in and zoom out.

3. Scroll left and right to see all the photos in the album.

4. Touch to share the picture with friends using Facebook, Twitter, Gmail, Email, Google+, Picasa (Google Photos), and Bluetooth.

5. Touch to return to the album view.

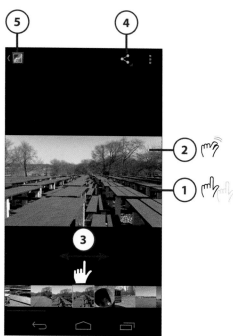

---

## Use Photo as Wallpaper or Contact Picture

While viewing a photo, touch the Menu button and choose Set As. You can choose to use the photo as a contact picture for one of your contacts, or use it as the wallpaper on the Home screen.

---

## Editing Pictures

You can edit a picture by adding special effects to it, enhancing it, or cropping it.

1. Touch the Menu button.

2. Touch Edit.

3. Touch to change the picture contrast.

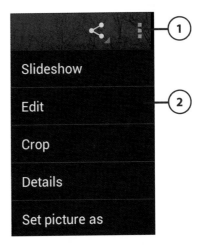

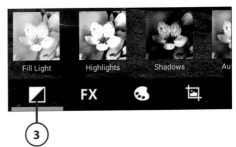

4. Touch to apply special effects to the photo, such as making it look like you used a fisheye lens when you took the picture, adding film graininess, and others .

5. Touch to change the color of the photo, including making it black and white.

6. Touch to crop the photo and do extra editing functions like flipping and rotating the photo.

7. Touch to undo changes you have made to a photo one-by-one. If you have made multiple changes, you can repeatedly touch the Undo icon until you have removed all changes.

8. Touch to redo a change that you have undone.

9. Touch to save your edited photo. Edited photos are placed in a new album called Edited so that the original photo remains intact.

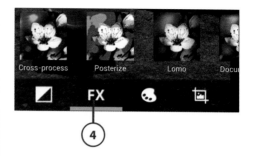

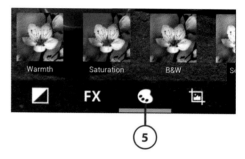

# Gallery Settings

1. Touch the Menu button.

2. Touch Settings.

3. Touch to enable or disable synchronizing photos over Wi-Fi only. If you uncheck this box, photo synchronization occurs even when you are using a cellular data network.

4. Touch a Google account to edit or remove it. After you touch an account, you see the next screen automatically.

5. Touch to enable or disable synchronization for all Google accounts.

6. Touch a Google account to edit or remove it.

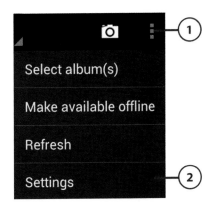

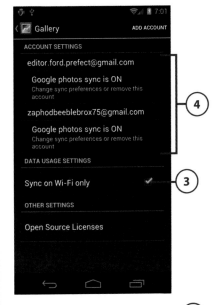

7. Touch to enable or disable synchronizing Google Photos for this Google account.

8. Touch the Menu button to reveal account actions.

9. Touch to remove the Google account.

10. Touch to manually synchronize the account.

11. Touch to save your changes and return to the previous screen.

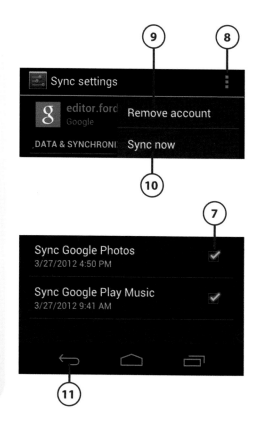

## Managing Photos with Your Computer

When you connect your Galaxy Nexus to a computer, you can move pictures back and forth manually. If you use an Apple Mac, you need some software called Android File Transfer. If you have not yet installed Android File Transfer, follow the installation steps in the "Prologue."

# Manual Picture Management

This section covers moving pictures using the Android File Transfer app if you are using a Mac or the media transfer functionality if you are using Windows.

1. Plug your Galaxy Nexus into your computer using the supplied USB cable.

2. Pull down the System Bar to reveal the USB Connected notification.

3. Touch the USB Connected notification.

4. Touch to check the box next to Media device (MTP), if it is not already checked.

## Moving Pictures (Mac OSX)

After your Galaxy Nexus is connected to your Mac, the Android File Transfer app automatically launches so you can browse the files on your phone as well as move or copy files between your Mac and your Galaxy Nexus.

**1.** Browse to your Galaxy Nexus to locate the pictures.

---

## Where Are the Pictures?

Pictures taken with the Galaxy Nexus camera are in the folder DCIM\Camera. All other pictures are in a folder called Pictures. Photos that you have edited are in a folder called Edited.

---

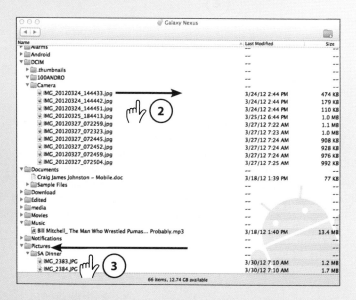

**2.** Drag one or more pictures from your Galaxy Nexus to a folder on your Mac.

**3.** Drag a folder filled with pictures on your Mac to the folder called Pictures on your Galaxy Nexus to create a new Photo Album.

**4.** Drag one or more pictures from your Mac to the Pictures folder on your Galaxy Nexus.

# Moving Pictures (Windows)

After your Galaxy Nexus is connected to your Windows computer and mounted, you can browse the Galaxy Nexus like any drive on your computer.

1. Click if you want to import the pictures automatically.

## Where Are the Pictures?

Pictures taken with the Galaxy Nexus camera are in the folder DCIM\Camera. All other pictures are in a folder called Pictures. Photos that you have edited are in a folder called Edited.

2. Click to open an Explorer view and see the files on your Galaxy Nexus.

3. Drag one or more pictures from your Galaxy Nexus to a folder on your PC.

4. Drag a folder filled with pictures on your PC to the folder called Pictures on your Galaxy Nexus to create a new Photo Album.

5. Drag one or more pictures from your PC to the Pictures folder on your Galaxy Nexus.

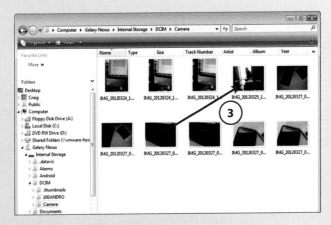

# Automatic Picture Management on a Mac

By setting your Galaxy Nexus to connect as a Camera, your Mac automatically opens iPhoto.

1. Plug your Galaxy Nexus into your computer using the supplied USB cable.

2. Pull down the System Bar to reveal the USB Connected notification.

3. Touch the USB Connected notification.

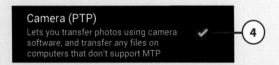

4. Touch to check the box next to Camera (PTP), if it is not already checked.

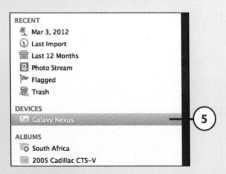

5. Your Galaxy Nexus appears in iPhoto under Devices so that you can import photos like you would with any other digital camera.

# Synchronizing Pictures Using Your Google Cloud

You can synchronize pictures to your Galaxy Nexus from your computer without even connecting your phone to your computer. Just use your Google account's built-in cloud service. All photo albums that you create in the cloud are automatically synchronized to your Galaxy Nexus.

1. Click Photos after you log in to Google on your desktop computer.

2. Click to see all the photos that have been automatically uploaded from your Galaxy Nexus to your Google Photos cloud account. When they display on the screen, you can download those pictures to your computer.

3. Click to manage your photo albums.

4. Click an existing photo album to open it, and add more photos to it from your computer.

5. Click to create a new photo album and add photos to it from your computer.

6. Type a name for your new photo album.

7. Click to browse your computer and choose photos to upload to the album.

8. Click to create the album.

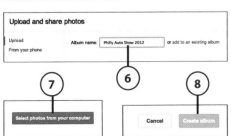

Browse for apps

Search for apps

In this chapter, you learn how to purchase and use Android applications on your Galaxy Nexus. Topics include the following:

→ Finding applications with Google Play
→ Purchasing applications
→ Keeping applications up to date

# 10

# Working with Android Applications

Your Galaxy Nexus comes with enough applications to make it a worthy smartphone. However, wouldn't it be great to play games, update your Facebook and Twitter statuses, or even keep a grocery list? Well, finding these types of applications is what the Google Play is for. Read on to learn about finding, purchasing, and maintaining applications.

## What Happened to Android Market?

Google recently updated the functionality of its store by adding the ability to not only find and purchase Android apps, but also to buy music, buy books, and rent movies. Because of this Android Market has been renamed to Google Play.

# Configuring Google Checkout

Before you start buying applications in the Google Play app, you must first sign up for a Google Checkout account. If you plan to only download free applications, you do not need a Google Checkout account.

1. From a desktop computer or your Galaxy Nexus, open the web browser and go to http://checkout.google.com.

2. Sign in using the Google account that you will be using to synchronize email to your Galaxy Nexus. See Chapter 1, "Contacts," or Chapter 5, "Emailing," for information about adding a Google account to your Galaxy Nexus.

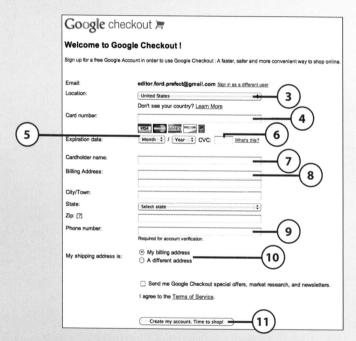

3. Choose your location. If your country is not listed, you have to use free applications until it's added to the list.

4. Enter your credit card number. This can also be a debit card that includes a Visa or MasterCard logo, also known as a check card, so that the funds are withdrawn from your checking account.

5. Select the month and year of the card's expiration date.

6. Enter the card's CVC number, which is also known as the security code. This is a three- or four-digit number that's printed on the back of your card.

7. Enter your name.

8.  Enter your billing address.

9.  Enter your phone number.

10. Although you don't need a mailing address for Google Play, you might want to choose an alternative delivery address for items you purchase from other online stores that use Google Checkout.

11. Click Create My Account when you're done with the form.

# Navigating Google Play

Android is the operating system that runs your Galaxy Nexus and, therefore, any applications that are made for your Galaxy Nexus need to run on Android. Google Play is a place where you can search for and buy Android applications.

1.  Touch the Play application icon.

**2.** Touch the Menu button to see Google Play actions.

**3.** Touch to see any apps you have already purchased or downloaded.

**4.** Touch to select which Google account you want to use when you use the Google Play store, if you have multiple Google accounts.

**5.** Touch to change the settings for Google Play. See the "Google Play Settings" section later in this chapter for more information.

**6.** Touch to browse all Android apps.

**7.** Touch to browse all Android games.

**8.** Touch to search Google Play.

# Downloading Free Applications

You don't have to spend money to get quality applications. Some of the best applications are actually free.

**1.** Touch the application you want to download.

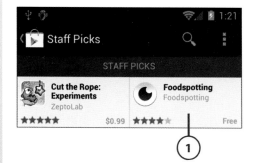

2. Scroll down to read the application features, reviews by other people who installed it, and information on the person or company who wrote the application.

3. Scroll left and right to see the app screenshots.

4. Touch Download to download the app.

5. Touch to accept the app permissions and proceed with the download.

## Beware of Permissions

Each time you download a free app or purchase an app from Google Play, you are prompted to accept the app permissions. App permissions are permissions the app wants to have to use features and functions on your Galaxy Nexus, such as access to the wireless network or access to your phone log. Pay close attention to the kinds of permissions each app is requesting and make sure they are appropriate for the type of functionality that the app provides. For example, an app that tests network speed will likely ask for permission to access your wireless network, but if it also asks to access your list of contacts, it might mean that the app is malware and just wants to steal your contacts.

**Permissions to your phone the app is requesting**

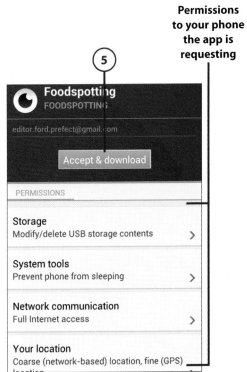

# Buying Applications

If an application is not free, the price is displayed next to the application icon. If you want to buy the application, remember that you need to already have a Google Checkout account. See the "Configuring Google Checkout" section earlier in the chapter for more information.

**1.** Touch the application you want to buy.

## What If the Currency Is Different?

When you browse applications in Google Play, you might see applications that have prices in foreign currencies, such as in euros. When you purchase an application, the currency is simply converted into your local currency using the exchange rate at the time of purchase.

**2.** Scroll down to read the application features, reviews by other people who installed it, and information on the person or company who wrote the application.

**3.** Scroll left and right to see all screenshots and app videos.

**4.** Touch the price to purchase the app.

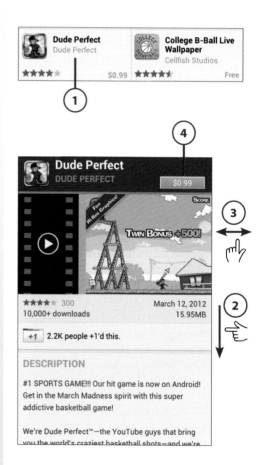

5. Touch to change the method of payment or add a new credit card.

6. Touch to purchase the app. You will receive an email from the Google Play after you purchase an app. The email serves as your invoice.

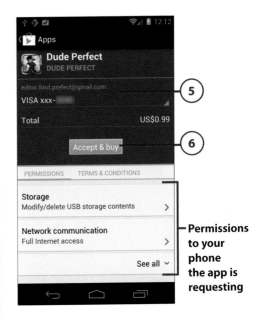

Permissions to your phone the app is requesting

# Managing Applications

Use the My Apps section of Google Play to update apps, delete them, or install apps that you have previously purchased.

1. Touch the Menu button.

2. Touch My Apps.

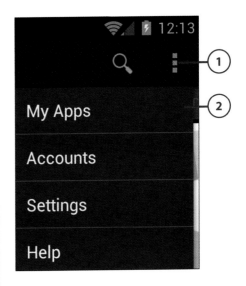

3. Touch All to see all apps that you have installed or might have previously installed.

4. Indicates the app is currently installed.

5. Indicates a free app that you previously installed but that is no longer installed. Touching the app enables you to install it again for free.

6. Indicates that the app can only be installed when you're connected to a Wi-Fi network as it is too large to be installed over the cellular data network.

7. Indicates an app that you previously purchased and installed but that is no longer installed. Touching the app allows you to install it again for free.

## Allow an App to Be Automatically Updated

When the developer of an app you have installed updates it to fix bugs or add new functionality, you are normally notified of this in the System Tray so that you can manually update the app. Google Play enables you to choose to have the app automatically updated without your intervention. To do this, open the My Apps screen and touch the app you want to update automatically. Check the box labeled Allow Automatic Updating. Be aware that if these updates occur while you are on a cellular data connection, your data limit for the month will be affected.

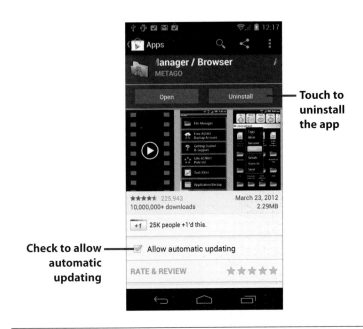

**Touch to uninstall the app**

**Check to allow automatic updating**

## Uninstalling an App

When you uninstall an app, you remove the app and its data from your Galaxy Nexus. Although the app no longer resides on your Galaxy Nexus, you can reinstall it as described in step 7 because the app remains tied to your Google account.

# Google Play Settings

1. Touch the Menu button.

2. Touch Settings

3. Touch to enable or disable notifications of app or game updates.

4. Touch to enable or disable setting all apps you install to automatically update themselves.

5. Touch to enable or disable forcing all app updates to occur only when you are connected to a Wi-Fi network.

6. Touch to enable or disable an app icon to appear on your Home screen for each app that you install.

7. Touch to clear the Google Play search history.

8. Scroll down to see more settings.

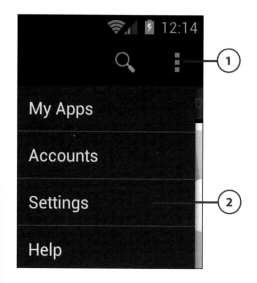

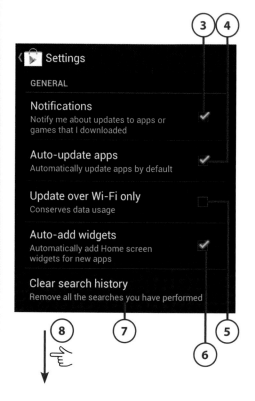

**9.** Touch to adjust or set your content filtering. Use this to filter out apps, movies, music, or books that you deem to be inappropriate.

**10.** Touch to set a PIN that must be typed in before changing the Google Play User Control settings (Content Filtering, PIN for purchases, and Set PIN).

**11.** Touch to use the PIN you set in step 10 for purchasing apps, music, books, or renting movies.

**12.** Touch to enable or disable having AdMob ads personalized based on your interests. AdMob ads normally show up in Free apps.

**13.** Touch to return to the main Google Play screen.

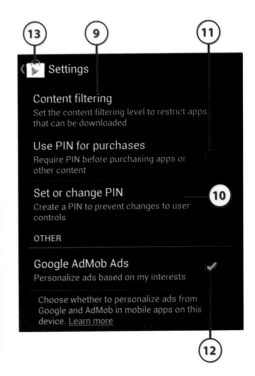

## Why Lock the User Settings?

Imagine if you buy a Galaxy Nexus for your child but want to make sure that he doesn't get to any undesirable content. First you set the content filtering to restrict the content visible in Google Play. Next you set the PIN so he can't change that setting. A similar idea goes for limiting purchases.

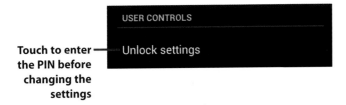

**Touch to enter the PIN before changing the settings**

## Accidentally Uninstall an Application?

What if you accidentally uninstall an application or you uninstalled an application in the past but now decide you'd like to use it again? To get the application back, go to the My Apps view in Google Play. Scroll to that application and touch it. Touch Install to re-install it.

# Keeping Applications Up to Date

Developers who write Android applications often update their applications to fix bugs or to add new features. With a few quick touches it is easy for you to update the applications that you have installed.

1. If an application you have installed has an update, you see the update notification in the notification bar.

2. Pull down the notification bar.

3. Touch the update notification.

4. Touch one of the applications that has an update available.

5. Touch Update.

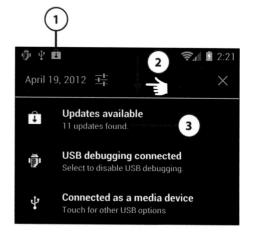

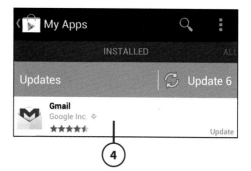

Live
Wallpaper

In this chapter, you learn how to customize your Galaxy Nexus to suit your needs and lifestyle. Topics include the following:

→ Wallpapers and live wallpapers
→ Replacing the keyboard
→ Sound and display settings
→ Setting region and language

# Customizing Your Galaxy Nexus

Your Galaxy Nexus arrives preconfigured to appeal to most buyers; however, you might want to change the way some of the features work or even personalize it to fit your mood or lifestyle. Luckily your Galaxy Nexus is customizable.

## Changing Your Wallpaper

Your Galaxy Nexus comes preloaded with a cool wallpaper. You can install other wallpapers, use live wallpapers that animate, and even use pictures in the Gallery application as your wallpaper.

1. Touch and hold on the Home screen.

2. Touch the type of wallpaper you want to use. Use the steps in one of the following three sections to select your wallpaper.

## Wallpaper from Gallery Pictures

You can use any picture in your Gallery as a wallpaper.

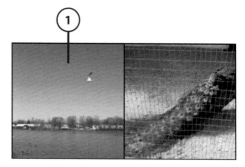

1. Select the photo you want to use as your wallpaper.

2. Move the crop box to the part of the photo you want to use.

3. Adjust the size of the crop box to include the part of the photo you want.

4. Touch OK to use the cropped portion of the photo as your wallpaper.

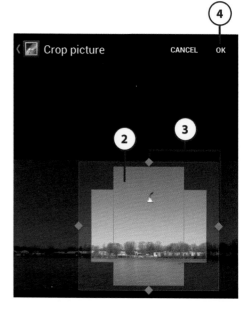

# Live Wallpaper

Live wallpaper is wallpaper with some intelligence behind it. It can be a cool animation or even an animation that keys off things such as the music you are playing on your Galaxy Nexus, or it can be something simple such as the time. There are some very cool live wallpapers in Google Play that you can install and use.

1. Touch the live wallpaper you want to use.

2. Touch to see and change the live wallpaper settings.

3. Touch Set Wallpaper to use the live wallpaper.

## Find More Wallpaper

You can find wallpaper or live wallpaper in Google Play. Open Google Play and search for "wallpaper" or "live wallpaper." Read more on how to use Google Play in Chapter 10, "Working with Android Applications."

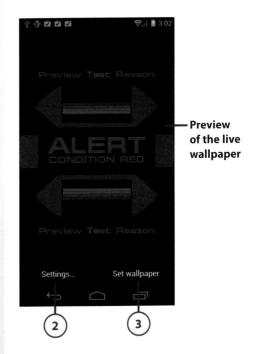

Preview of the live wallpaper

## Wallpaper

Choose a static wallpaper.

1. Scroll left and right to see all of the wallpapers.

2. Touch a wallpaper to preview it.

3. Touch Set Wallpaper to use the wallpaper.

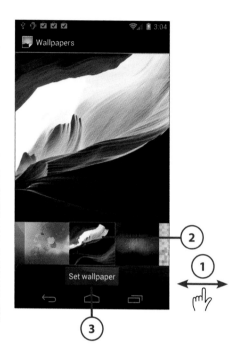

# Changing Your Keyboard

If you find it hard to type on the standard Galaxy Nexus keyboard, or you just want to make it look better, you can install replacement keyboards. You can download free or purchase replacement keyboards from the Google Play. Make sure you install a keyboard before following these steps.

1. Touch Settings.

2. Touch Language & Input.

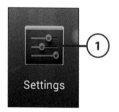

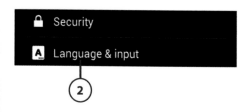

3. Check the box next to a keyboard you have previously installed (GO Keyboard, in this case) to enable that keyboard.

4. Touch Default to change the default keyboard to the one you have just enabled.

## Do Your Research

When you choose a different keyboard in step 3, the Galaxy Nexus gives you a warning telling you that nonstandard keyboards have the potential for capturing everything you type. Do your research on any keyboards before you download and install them.

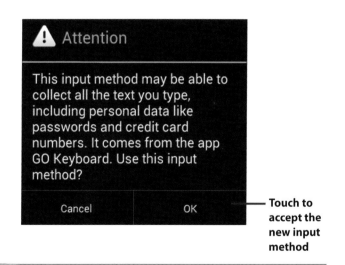

**Touch to accept the new input method**

5.  Touch the name of your new keyboard to select it.

## What Can You Do with Your New Keyboard?

Keyboards you buy in Google Play can do many things. They can change the key layout, change the color and style of the keys, offer different methods of text input, and even enable you to use an old T9 predictive input keyboard that you may have become used to when using an old "dumb phone" that only had a numeric keypad.

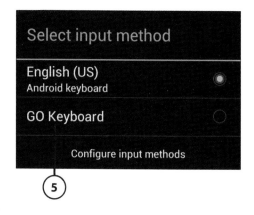

# Adding Widgets to Your Home Screens

Some applications that you install come with widgets that you can place on your Home screens. These widgets normally display real-time information such as stocks, weather, time, and Facebook feeds. Your Galaxy Nexus also comes preinstalled with some widgets. Here is how to add and manage widgets.

## Adding a Widget

Your Galaxy Nexus should come preinstalled with some widgets, but you might also have some extra ones that were added when you installed other applications. Here is how to add those widgets to your Home screens.

1.  Touch the Launcher.

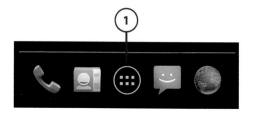

2. Touch Widgets.

3. Touch and hold a widget to move it to the Home screen. Keep holding the widget as you move to step 4.

4. Position the widget where you want it on the Home screen.

5. Drag the widget between sections of the home screen.

6. Release your finger to place the widget.

## How Many Widgets Can I Fit?

Each part of the Home screen is divided into four blocks across and four blocks down. When you see the widgets in step 2 you'll notice that each one shows its size in blocks across and down. From that you can prejudge if a widget will fit on the screen you want it to be on, but it also helps you position it in step 3.

**Widget's size**

**Scroll left and right to see all widgets**

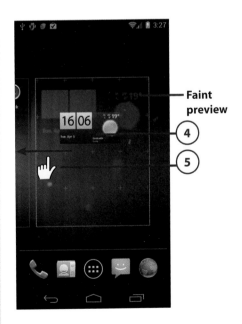

**Faint preview**

# Remove, Move, or Resize a Widget

Sometimes you want to remove a widget, resize it, or move it around. Here is how.

1. Touch and hold the widget until you see a blue shadow, but continue to hold the widget.

2. Drag the widget to the trash can to remove it.

3. Drag the widget around the screen or drag it between sections of the Home screen to reposition it.

4. Release the widget to reveal the resize box.

5. Drag the sides to resize the widget.

6. Touch anywhere on the Home screen to stop resizing.

# Language

If you move to another country or want to change the language used by your Galaxy Nexus, you can do so with a few touches.

1. Touch Settings.

2. Touch Language & Input.

3. Touch Language.

4. Touch the language you want to switch to.

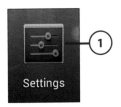

---

## What Obeys the Language Setting?

When you switch your Galaxy Nexus to use a different language you immediately notice that all standard applications and the Galaxy Nexus menus switch to the new language. Even some third-party applications honor the language switch. However many third-party applications ignore the language setting on the Galaxy Nexus. So you might open a third-party application and find that all of its menus are still in English.

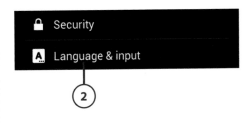

**Scroll to see all languages**

# Accessibility Settings

Your Galaxy Nexus includes built-in settings to assist people who might otherwise have difficulty using some features of the device. The Galaxy Nexus has the ability to provide alternative feedback such as vibration, sound, and even speaking of menus.

1. Touch Settings.

2. Touch Accessibility.

3. Touch to enable or disable TalkBack. When enabled, TalkBack speaks everything, including menus.

4. Touch to enable or disable large text.

5. Touch to enable a feature where the Power button can be used to end phone calls.

6. Touch to enable automatic screen rotation. When disabled, the screen will not rotate between portrait and landscape modes.

7. Touch to change how long you have to hold when you perform a touch and hold on the screen.

8. Touch to allow or disallow Google web scripts that make websites more accessible.

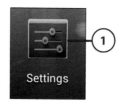

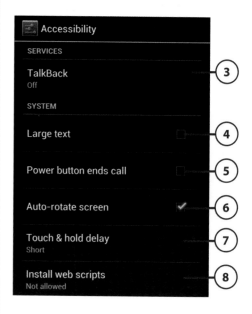

# Sound Settings

You can change the volume for games, ringtones, and alarms; change the default ringtone and notification sound; plus control what system sounds are used.

1. Touch Settings.

2. Touch Sound.

3. Touch to change the volume for games and media such as videos and music, ringtones and notifications, and alarms.

4. Touch to choose when your Galaxy Nexus must vibrate. You can choose Always, Never, Only in Silent Mode, or Only When Not in Silent Mode.

5. Touch to enable or disable Silent Mode.

6. Touch to choose the default phone ringtone.

7. Touch to choose the default notification ringtone.

8. Touch to enable or disable dial pad touch tones.

9. Touch to enable or disable the touch sounds that play when you touch something on the screen or a menu.

10. Scroll down for more settings.

11. Touch to enable or disable the screen lock sound that plays when your Galaxy Nexus locks the screen after the inactivity timeout.

12. Touch to enable or disable vibrating on touch. When enabled, your Galaxy Nexus vibrates quickly when you touch the screen.

# Display Settings

You can change the screen brightness or set it to automatic, change the wallpaper, change how long to wait before your Galaxy Nexus will go to sleep, the size of the font used, and whether to use the Pulse notification light.

1. Touch Settings.

2. Touch Display.

3. Touch to change the screen brightness manually or set it to automatic. When on automatic, your Galaxy Nexus uses the built-in light sensor to adjust the brightness based on the light levels in the room.

Settings

4. Touch to change the Wallpaper. See more about how to change the wallpaper earlier in this chapter.

5. Touch to enable or disable the auto-rotate screen function. When this setting is enabled, as you tilt your Galaxy Nexus onto its side the screen automatically switches to landscape mode.

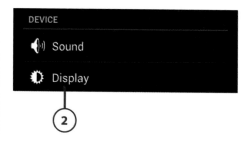

6. Touch to choose how many minutes of inactivity must pass before your Galaxy Nexus puts the screen to sleep.

7. Touch to choose the font size of all text used.

8. Touch to enable or disable using the Pulse notification light when you receive a new notification. The Pulse notification light is under the screen.

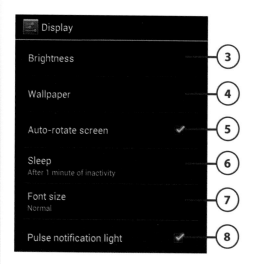

See your battery
usage trends

In this chapter, you learn how to maintain your Galaxy Nexus and solve problems. Topics include the following:

→ Updating Android
→ Optimizing battery life
→ Identifying battery-hungry applications
→ Caring for your Galaxy Nexus

# Maintaining Galaxy Nexus and Solving Problems

Every so often Google releases new versions of Android that have bug fixes and new features. In this chapter you find out how to upgrade your Galaxy Nexus to a new version of Android and how to tackle common problem-solving issues and general maintenance of your Galaxy Nexus.

## Updating Android

New releases of Android are always exciting because they add new features, fix bugs, and tweak the user interface. Here is how to update your Galaxy Nexus.

### Update Information

Updates to Android are not on a set schedule. The update messages appear as you turn on your Galaxy Nexus, and they remain in the notification bar until you install the update. If you touch Install Later, your Galaxy Nexus reminds you that there's an update every 30 minutes. Sometimes people like to wait to see if there are any bugs that need to be worked out before they update, so it is up to you.

1. Pull down the System Bar.

## Manually Check for Updates

If you think there should be an update for your Galaxy Nexus, but you have not yet received the onscreen notification, you can check manually by touching Settings, About Phone, and System Updates. If there are updates, they are listed on this screen.

2. Touch System Update Available.

3. Touch Install Now.

4. Touch Restart & Install. Your Galaxy Nexus updates and reboots.

Indicates a system update is available

Touch to install later

# Optimizing Battery Life

The battery in your Galaxy Nexus is a lithium ion battery that provides good battery life when you take care of it. Changing the way you use your Galaxy Nexus helps prolong the battery's life, which gives you more hours in a day to use your phone.

## Looking After the Battery

There are specific actions you can take to correctly care for the battery in your Galaxy Nexus. Caring for your battery helps it last longer.

- Try to avoid discharging the battery completely. Fully discharging the battery too frequently harms the battery. Instead, try to keep it partially charged at all times (except as described in the next step).

- To avoid a false battery level indication on your Galaxy Nexus, let the battery fully discharge about every 30 charges. Lithium-ion batteries do not have "memory" like older battery technologies; the battery meter gives a false reading if you don't fully discharge the battery every 30 charges.

- Do not leave your Galaxy Nexus in a hot car or out in the sun anywhere, including on the beach, as this can damage the battery and make it lose charge quickly. Leaving your Galaxy Nexus lying in the snow or in extreme cold also damages the battery.

- Consider having multiple chargers. For example, you could have one at home, one at work, and maybe one at a client's site. This enables you to always keep your Galaxy Nexus charged.

# Determining What Is Using the Battery

Your Galaxy Nexus enables you to see exactly what apps and system processes are using your battery. Having access to this information can help you alter your usage patterns and reduce the battery drain.

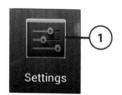

Settings

1. Touch Settings.

2. Touch Battery.

3. Touch to manually refresh the display.

4. Touch an app or Android service to see more details about it, including how much time it has been active, how much processor (CPU) time it has used, and how much data it has sent and received (if applicable).

5. Touch the battery graph for more details.

Storage

Battery

Battery

100% - Charging (USB)

15h 4m 43s on battery

Android OS    36%

Phone idle    26%

Screen    14%

6. Mobile Network Signal indicates the mobile network signal strength through the battery graph's time span.

7. GPS On indicates when the GPS radio was being used through the battery graph's time span.

8. WiFi indicates when the Wi-Fi radio was being used through the battery graph's time span.

9. Awake indicates when your Galaxy Nexus was awake through the battery graph's time span.

10. Screen On indicates when your Galaxy Nexus screen was on through the battery graph's time span.

11. Charging indicates when your Galaxy Nexus was charging through the battery graph's time span.

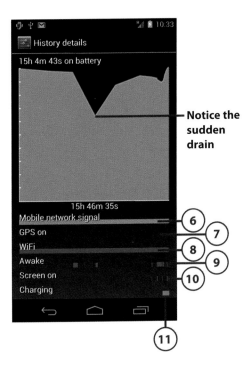

**Notice the sudden drain**

## How Can Seeing Battery Drain Help?

If you look at the way your battery has been draining, you can see when the battery was draining the fastest, and you should be able to remember what apps you were using at that time or what you were doing on your Galaxy Nexus. Based on that you can either change your usage habits or maybe come to the conclusion that a specific app you are using is misbehaving.

# Applications and Memory

When applications run on your Galaxy Nexus, they all run in a specific memory space, which is limited to 1GB. Although Android tries to do a good job of managing this memory, sometimes you have to step in and close an app that is consuming too much memory.

1. Touch Settings.

2. Touch Apps.

3. Touch Running to see only apps that are currently running.

4. The graph shows how much memory is being used by running apps and cached processes compared to how much space is free.

5. Touch an app to see more information about it.

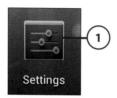

Touch to see processes that Android is caching

6. Touch Stop if you believe the app is misbehaving.

7. Touch to report an app to Google. You might want to do this if it is misbehaving, using up too many resources, or you suspect it of stealing data.

8. Indicates the processes that are being used by this app.

## When to Manually Stop an App

After you have been using your Galaxy Nexus for a while, you'll become familiar with how long it takes to do certain tasks such as typing, navigating menus, and so on. If you notice your Galaxy Nexus becoming slow or not behaving the way you think it should, the culprit could be a new application you recently installed. Because Android never quits applications on its own, that new application continues running in the background and causing your Galaxy Nexus to slow down. This is when it is useful to manually stop an app.

# Reigning In Your Data Usage

If you are worried that you might use too much data each month you can set a usage limit on your Galaxy Nexus and even prevent apps from using data while they are running in the background.

1. Touch Settings.

2. Touch Data Usage.

3. Touch to enable or disable mobile data limits. When this is enabled, your Galaxy Nexus automatically cuts off all mobile data usage when the limit you set in step 5 is reached.

4. Touch to set the dates for your cellular carrier's monthly billing cycle.

5. Slide up and down to select the mobile data limit you want to impose. This may or may not match your cellular data plan limit.

6. Slide up and down to set a data usage warning threshold. When you reach or pass this threshold, you see a warning in the System Bar.

7. Touch an app to see more details about its data usage and to control how it uses data in the background.

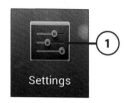

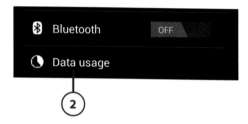

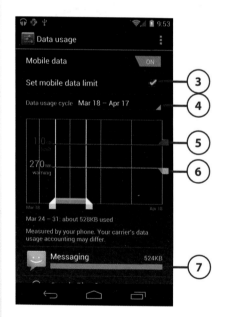

## Background Data Limits

When you touch an app to see its data usage (step 7 of the preceding task), you can also limit its usage when it is in the background. When an app is in the background, it means it is running although you are not using it, and it might still be using data.

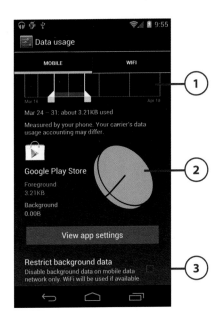

1. Shows the specific data usage for this app.

2. Shows the breakdown of data usage in foreground and background.

3. Touch to restrict the app from using data while it is in the background.

# Caring for Galaxy Nexus Exterior

Because you need to touch your Galaxy Nexus screen to use it, it picks up oils and other residue from your hands. You also might get dirt on other parts of the phone. Here is how to clean your Galaxy Nexus.

1. Wipe the screen with a microfiber cloth. You can purchase these in most electronic stores, or you can use the one that came with your sunglasses.

2. To clean dirt off other parts of your phone, wipe it with a damp cloth. Never use soap or chemicals on your Galaxy Nexus as they can damage it.

3. When inserting the Micro-USB connector, try not to force it in the wrong way. If you damage the pins inside your Galaxy Nexus, you will not be able to charge it.

# Getting Help with Your Galaxy Nexus

There are many resources on the Internet where you can get help with your Galaxy Nexus.

1. Visit the Official Google website at http://www.android.com.

2. Check out some Android blogs:

    - Android Central at http://www.androidcentral.com/

    - Android Guys at http://www.androidguys.com/

    - Androinica at http://androinica.com/

3. Contact me. I don't mind answering your questions, so visit my official *My Samsung Galaxy Nexus* book site at http://www.CraigsBooks.info.

# Index

# J-K

# L

# Y-Z

# Try Safari Books Online FREE for 15 days
## Get online access to Thousands of Books and Videos

> ## Feed your brain
> Gain unlimited access to thousands of books and videos about technology, digital media and professional development from O'Reilly Media, Addison-Wesley, Microsoft Press, Cisco Press, McGraw Hill, Wiley, WROX, Prentice Hall, Que, Sams, Apress, Adobe Press and other top publishers.

> ## See it, believe it
> Watch hundreds of expert-led instructional videos on today's hottest topics.

## WAIT, THERE'S MORE!

> ## Gain a competitive edge
> Be first to learn about the newest technologies and subjects with Rough Cuts pre-published manuscripts and new technology overviews in Short Cuts.

> ## Accelerate your project
> Copy and paste code, create smart searches that let you know when new books about your favorite topics are available, and customize your library with favorites, highlights, tags, notes, mash-ups and more.

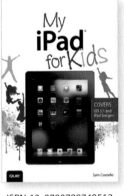

Your purchase of *My Samsung Galaxy Nexus* includes access to a free online edition for 45 days through the **Safari Books Online** subscription service. Nearly every Que book is available online through **Safari Books Online**, along with thousands of books and videos from publishers such as Addison-Wesley Professional, Cisco Press, Exam Cram, IBM Press, O'Reilly Media, Prentice Hall, Sams, and VMware Press.

**Safari Books Online** is a digital library providing searchable, on-demand access to thousands of technology, digital media, and professional development books and videos from leading publishers. With one monthly or yearly subscription price, you get unlimited access to learning tools and information on topics including mobile app and software development, tips and tricks on using your favorite gadgets, networking, project management, graphic design, and much more.

## Activate your FREE Online Edition at
## informit.com/safarifree

**STEP 1:**   Enter the coupon code: TMIHFAA.

**STEP 2:**   New Safari users, complete the brief registration form.
Safari subscribers, just log in.

If you have difficulty registering on Safari or accessing the online edition,
please e-mail customer-service@safaribooksonline.com